Narrative Research

BLOOMSBURY RESEARCH METHODS

Edited by Mark Elliot and Jessica Nina Lester

The Bloomsbury Research Methods series provides authoritative introductions to key and emergent research methods across a range of disciplines.

Each book introduces the key elements of a particular method and/or methodology and includes examples of its application. Written in an accessible style by leading experts in the field, this series is an innovative pedagogical and research resource.

Also available in the series

Community Studies, Graham Crow
Diary Method, Ruth Bartlett and Christine Milligan
Embodied Inquiry, Jennifer Leigh and Nicole Brown
GIS, Nick Bearman
Inclusive Research, Melanie Nind
Mixed Methods Research, Donna M. Mertens
Online Research, Tristram Hooley and Rachel Buchanan
Qualitative Interviewing, 2nd edition, Rosalind Edwards and Janet Holland
Qualitative Longitudinal Research, Bren Neale
Quantitative Longitudinal Data Analysis, Vernon Gayle and Paul Lambert
Rhythmanalysis, Dawn Lyon
Social Network Analysis, John Scott
Vignette Research, Evi Agostini, Michael Schratz and Irma Eloff

Forthcoming in the series

Anecdote Research, Hans Karl Peterlini and Gabriele Rathgeb
Statistical Modelling in R, Kevin Ralston, Vernon Gayle, Roxanne Connelly and Chris Playford

Narrative Research

Research Methods

MOLLY ANDREWS, MARK DAVIS,
CIGDEM ESIN,
BARBARA HARRISON,
LARS-CHRISTER HYDÉN,
MARGARETA HYDÉN,
AURA LOUNASMAA AND
CORINNE SQUIRE

BLOOMSBURY ACADEMIC
LONDON • NEW YORK • OXFORD • NEW DELHI • SYDNEY

BLOOMSBURY ACADEMIC
Bloomsbury Publishing Plc
50 Bedford Square, London, WC1B 3DP, UK
1385 Broadway, New York, NY 10018, USA
29 Earlsfort Terrace, Dublin 2, Ireland

BLOOMSBURY, BLOOMSBURY ACADEMIC and the Diana logo are trademarks of
Bloomsbury Publishing Plc

First published in Great Britain 2014

This edition published 2025

Copyright © Molly Andrews, Mark Davis, Cigdem Esin, Barbara Harrison,
Lars-Christer Hydén, Margareta Hydén, Aura Lounasmaa and Corinne Squire, 2025

Molly Andrews, Mark Davis, Cigdem Esin, Barbara Harrison, Lars-Christer Hydén, Margareta
Hydén, Aura Lounasmaa and Corinne Squire have asserted their right under the Copyright,
Designs and Patents Act, 1988, to be identified as Authors of this work.

Cover design: Charlotte James
Cover image © shuoshu / iStock

All rights reserved. No part of this publication may be reproduced or transmitted in any
form or by any means, electronic or mechanical, including photocopying, recording, or
any information storage or retrieval system, without prior permission in writing from the
publishers.

Bloomsbury Publishing Plc does not have any control over, or responsibility for, any
third-party websites referred to or in this book. All internet addresses given in this book were
correct at the time of going to press. The author and publisher regret any inconvenience
caused if addresses have changed or sites have ceased to exist, but can accept no
responsibility for any such changes.

A catalogue record for this book is available from the British Library.

Library of Congress Cataloging-in-Publication Data
Names: Andrews, Molly, author.
Title: Narrative research : research methods / Molly Andrews, Mark Davis,
Barbara Harrison, Lars-Christer Hyde'n, Margareta Hyde'n,
Aura Lounasmaa and Corinne Squire.
Description: New York, NY : Bloomsbury Academic, 2024. |
Series: Bloomsbury research methods |
Includes bibliographical references and index.
Identifiers: LCCN 2024026863 (print) | LCCN 2024026864 (ebook) |
ISBN 9781350319042 (hardback) | ISBN 9781350319035 (paperback) |
ISBN 9781350319066 (epub) | ISBN 9781350319059 (epdf)
Subjects: LCSH: Social sciences–Research–Methodology.
Classification: LCC H61.295 .A55 2024 (print) | LCC H61.295 (ebook) |
DDC 300.72/1–dc23/eng/20240816
LC record available at https://lccn.loc.gov/2024026863
LC ebook record available at https://lccn.loc.gov/2024026864

ISBN: HB: 978-1-3503-1904-2
PB: 978-1-3503-1903-5
ePDF: 978-1-3503-1905-9
ePUB: 978-1-3503-1906-6

Series: Bloomsbury Research Methods

Typeset by Newgen KnowledgeWorks Pvt. Ltd., Chennai, India
Printed and bound in Great Britain

To find out more about our authors and books visit www.bloomsbury.com
and sign up for our newsletters.

'*Narrative Research* provides an engaging, accessible introduction to narrative research in social sciences. It includes inspiring examples that illustrate how to do narrative research and why it can be exciting, challenging, and rewarding. Although it focuses on social sciences, it is useful for anyone interested in narrative studies across disciplines.'
Hanna Meretoja, University of Turku, Finland.

'*Narrative Research* offers diverse and engaging approaches to exploring individuals and society. This book centers on the vivid voices of field experts with diverse experiences and academic backgrounds. This book is not merely an introduction to the meaning of narrative, *narrative research* methods, or practices. It seeks fundamental reflection on human and social issues. Narrative Research consists of engaging subjects, entertaining stories, and meaningful structures. This book is not something to be read quickly. Instead, it offers a serious and systematic approach for anyone seeking reflection on themselves and humanity.'
Yohan Goh, Yonsei University, South Korea.

'Both experienced and novice researchers will hugely benefit from this read. The book sketches the broad co-ordinates of narrative research, offering an expansive scope including numerous examples from a range of disciplines and applications of narrative work. The depth and breadth of examples, including many from the majority world, offer an expansive view of the exciting developments in the field that disrupt its 'authority' as 'expertise' located in the minority world. The book offers a reading of narrative research that is hugely relevant for our contemporary global context where questions of social justice, ethics and re-humanisation should take front and center stage. I strongly recommend this accessible and illuminating read!'
Floretta Boonzaier, University of Cape Town, South Africa.

'This book has much to offer researchers at all career stages who are seeking to incorporate narrative methods into their research. Apart from an overview of concepts essential to doing narrative research, the chapters also consider the ways in which narratives may be expressed beyond written and spoken modes, and examples of challenging social issues that can benefit from narrative research.

Useful approaches and tools are presented alongside a range of different datasets as demonstrations of how this endeavour may be done.'
Charity Lee, Universiti Malaya, Malaysia.

'This comprehensive introduction to conducting narrative research in the social sciences reflects the unique sensitivity, wisdom, and responsibility gained from the authors' extensive experience in the field. They invite you on a step-by-step journey filled with rich examples and practical tools, providing the valuable research companion they wished they had when they started. No matter where you are, this book will equip you with the resources you need to navigate your own path in narrative research.'
Oriana Bernasconi, Alberto Hurtado University, Chile.

To Cigdem, for whom narrative research was always a thoughtful, relational and creative process of living, and who we miss every day of our lives.

CONTENTS

About the authors x
Series Editors' Foreword xii

1. What is narrative research? Starting out 1
2. What's the story? Five contemporary issues in narrative research 29
3. Narratives in social research: Researching narratives across media 43
4. Narratives in social research: Researching narratives, power and resistance 59
5. The uses of narrative research 81
6. Challenges in narrative research 105

Further Readings and Resources 127
References 139
Index 159

ABOUT THE AUTHORS

Molly Andrews is Honorary Professor of Political Psychology at the Social Research Institute, University College London, UK, Adjunct Professor at the Graduate Center of the City University of New York and a co-director of the Association of Narrative Research and Practice (ANRP). Her books include *Lifetimes of Commitment: Aging, Politics, Psychology, Shaping History: Narratives of Political Change* and *Narrative Imagination and Everyday Life*. She serves on the editorial board of six journals, which are published in four countries, and her publications have appeared in Chinese, German, Swedish, Spanish, French, Czech, German, Norwegian and Finnish. For more information, see https://www.mollyandrews.co.uk.

Mark Davis is Professor in the School of Social Sciences, Monash University, Australia. His publications include *Selling Immunity: Self, Culture and Economy in Healthcare and Medicine* and *Pandemic, Publics and Narrative*, co-authored with Davina Lohm. For more information, see https://research.monash.edu/en/persons/mark-davis.

Cigdem Esin was a narrative researcher and co-director of the Association of Narrative Research and Practice – previously the Centre for Narrative Research. She first arrived at CNR to do her PhD in 2004. Before her untimely death in 2022, Cigdem taught Psychosocial Studies at the University of East London, UEL. Her key interests were in the interconnections between micro- and macro-narratives, narrative positioning and narratives in relation to constructions of the self. We have retained and updated Cigdem's writing in this book, drawing on her work after the first edition (Esin, 2017; Esin and Lounasmaa, 2020).

ABOUT THE AUTHORS

Barbara Harrison is Emerita Professor of Sociology at the University of East London and Visiting Lecturer in the Professional Doctorate Programmes at Tavistock and Portman NHS Trust. She is the editor of the four-volume *Life Story Research*. She has also published widely on visual sociology.

Lars-Christer Hydén is Professor Emeritus of Social Psychology at Linköping University, Sweden. His research concerns how people living with dementia engage in social interaction using multimodal communicative resources as a way to sustain and negotiate everyday life and a sense of self. He has been especially interested in how people living with dementia engage in storytelling. His publications include *Entangled Narratives: Collaborative Storytelling and the Re-imagining of Dementia*.

Margareta Hydén is Professor Emerita in Social Work at Linköping University, Sweden, and Affiliated Professor in Criminology at Stockholm University, Sweden. Her recent work focuses on social networks' responses to interpersonal violence, children's narratives of witnessing violence in the family and narratives of sensitive topics. For more information, see https://www.su.se/profiles/hyden.

Aura Lounasmaa is a postdoctoral researcher in the Space and Political Agency Research Group at the University of Tampere, where she researches embodied encounters in asylum seeking. She is the vice-chair of the Narrare Centre for Interdisciplinary Narrative Studies and a co-director of the ANRP Association for Narrative Research and Practice (formerly CNR). In 2016–2022 she directed the Erasmus+ funded OLIve course for refugees and asylum seekers at the University of East London, shortlisted for the *Times Highered* 2022 International Collaboration of the Year award. She has published about refugee education and arts-based narrative methods, and many of her publications feature co-authorships with refugee students.

Corinne Squire is co-director of ANRP and Chair in Global Inequalities, University of Bristol. She is also an associate researcher at Witwatersrand University, Johannesburg, South Africa, and holds visiting positions at UCL, Manchester University and Edinburgh University. Recent publications include *Stories Changing Lives and Researching Family Narratives*, co-authored with Julia Brannen and Ann Phoenix.

SERIES EDITORS' FOREWORD

The idea behind this book series is a simple one: to provide concise and accessible introductions to frequently used research methodologies and methods, as well as to current issues in research methodology. Books in the series have been written by experts in their fields with a request to write about their subject for a broad audience.

The series has been developed through a partnership between Bloomsbury and the UK's National Centre for Research Methods (NCRM). The original 'what is' series sprang from the eponymous strand at NCRM's popular Research Methods Festivals, which began in 2004 and moved online in 2021 for its ninth run.

This relaunched series reflects changes in the research landscape, embracing research methods innovation and interdisciplinarity. Methodological innovation is the order of the day, and the books provide updates to the latest developments while still maintaining an emphasis on accessibility to a wide audience. The format allows researchers who are new to a field to gain an insight into its key features, while also providing a useful update on recent developments for people who have had some prior acquaintance with it. All readers should find it helpful to be taken through the discussion of key terms, the history of how the method or methodological issue has developed, and the assessment of the strengths and possible weaknesses of the approach through analysis of illustrative examples.

In *Narrative Research*, Molly Andrews, Mark Davis, Cigdem Esin, Barbara Harrison, Lars-Christer Hydén, Margareta Hydén, Aura Lounasmaa and Corinne Squire offer a state-of-the-art overview of narrative research methods and, in so doing, provide a contemporary perspective on what this methodology affords and how it can be enacted. Andrews et al. do not simply provide a discussion of the various meanings of 'narrative' but foreground the question: 'What do narrative researchers do?' As such, the authors – who are all members of the Association of Narrative Research and Practice (previously, the Centre for Narrative Research) – provide both a rich and detailed background from which readers might design and envisage a narrative study.

Across the six chapters, the authors explain the meaning(s) of narratives and narrative research by including rich examples. While they note that there are many fields within the social sciences that use narrative methods, they clarify that what they provide in the book is situated within one perspective. Specifically, this book offers perspectives on narrative research that lie primarily 'in the minority world', places emphasis on working alongside participants and foregrounds social justice. As sociologists and psychologists, the authors bring a wealth of diverse experiences to their writing, providing readers with concrete examples of how to design and carry out a narrative study.

Importantly, the final chapter of the book overviews some of the key challenges of narrative research. This chapter offers a roadmap for critical considerations that readers must consider as they conduct narrative research. For instance, the authors pose the question: 'Are there instructions for doing narrative research?' They aptly note that while there are no strict instructions, there are certainly 'basic research steps' that provide researchers with a framework within which to carry out narrative research. Andrews and colleagues very usefully unpack how this framework can be envisioned, further offering concrete guidance for readers pursuing narrative methods.

While the books within this series do not provide information about their subject matter down to a fine level of detail, they do equip readers with a sense of the reasons why a methodology is worth careful consideration. This book is no exception. Indeed, the authors provide a compelling and important starting point for readers interested in using up narrative methods.

Jessica Nina Lester and Mark Elliot

CHAPTER 1

What is narrative research? Starting out

A. Introducing narrative research

Narrative research is an increasingly common and popular approach in social sciences. It promises new fields of inquiry, creative addresses to persistent problems, ways to establish links with other disciplines such as cultural and literary studies, enhanced possibilities of applying research, and better understandings and practices of the politics of research. This book introduces you, step by step and with examples, to narrative research in the social sciences. It will show you a range of approaches to narrative research, their strengths and limits. It will do this by drawing on work from a variety of social science disciplines, in theoretical and applied fields, across diverse topics – pandemics and climate emergency, national memory, wealth inequalities, forced migration, gender-based violence, aging and disabilities, everyday photography and digital lives. It will also alert you to some of the limitations and issues in narrative research and provide suggestions for dealing with them.

Narrative Research provides a broad but necessarily incomplete picture, zooming in on some areas to give you a sense of how narrative research can work, rather than providing a full overview. Narrative research 'overviews' are never complete, because they are always views from a particular standpoint. Those standpoints come from specific disciplines and histories, usually those of the minority world (a term that is more accurate than 'Global North' or 'developed world' and that also recognizes the strength of the majority world, as Alam (2008) has argued). But narrative research overall is much more expansive than this in its extent and engagements.

The standpoints of this book's authors lie mostly in the minority world or 'global north'. We also share with most narrative researchers an interest in understanding people's thinking, feeling and actions through narratives. As well, like many contemporary narrative researchers, we are interested in addressing the relations between narrative and action; researching alongside participants; bringing together theory and method, research and practice. We hope to do narrative research, as Floretta Boonzaier has described it, 'in the interests of social justice ... and rehumanising' (2019: 488). *Narrative Research*, a new edition of an earlier text (Squire et al., 2014), aims to reflect such contemporary commitments.

'Narrative' is a term used widely and sometimes contradictorily in everyday life, as well as in literary studies, cultural studies, psychoanalytic studies, history, fine art, socio-legal studies, criminology, philosophy, management, computer game studies and film theory. Our book draws on these different fields; it cannot do justice to all of them or resolve their differences. It focuses on contemporary narrative work within social research. The book's authors are sociologists and psychologists. We have also published in the fields of social work, health, education, politics, sociology, human geography and psychotherapy. We have personal and academic associations with Sweden, the UK, Turkey, Finland, South Africa and the United States. The book's examples draw on these involvements and concerns.

Narrative Research assumes no expertise beyond your history of making and thinking about narratives. We hope you will be able to build up your understanding, engaging with more issues and perspectives, across the course of the book. Throughout, we base our arguments on specific narratives that demonstrate the points we are making. In the early chapters, we also list new terms as we introduce them to give you an idea of the vocabulary of narrative research.

The researchers who wrote this book are members of the Association of Narrative Research and Practice (previously, the Centre for Narrative Research). We all have strong interests in doing narrative research, but none of us knew how to do it at first. It was difficult to find out what to do, to choose between the many options available and to justify our choices. Narrative research was exciting and fruitful, producing many new insights, but it threw up problems at every step. We have tried to write the book that we would have liked to have beside us as we started doing narrative research ourselves.

The first chapter discusses what narrative research is and definitions of narrative; how narrative researchers go about doing narrative research; where we find narratives; and where narrative research itself comes from.

Chapter 2 introduces you to some important debates in narrative research and concerns that cut across the field. These debates are about narratives versus stories; coherence and incoherence in narratives; the co-construction and performance of narratives; narratives and reflexivity; and counter-narratives.

In Chapters 3 and 4, we provide some case studies of narrative research. Chapter 3 provides three short summaries of narrative research across different media: the body, visual media and social media. How narratives work across and between media is a strong concern of contemporary research. Chapter 4 presents three case studies of narrative research: violence and abuse; sexualities and power; and politics. This chapter speaks to narrative research's concerns with personal and political understanding and action.

Chapter 5 discusses the uses of narrative research. What possibilities does it offer to us as researchers; what are its limitations? The chapter considers how narrative research addresses little-known phenomena and whether and how it allows a 'voice' for those phenomena; what it tells us about people's lives; and narrative research's relations to social and political worlds. It then briefly provides examples of narrative research's usefulness in two areas where it is frequently used: health research and research on difficult or 'sensitive' topics.

Finally, in Chapter 6, we summarize some guidelines and challenges for narrative research. We end with some thoughts about ethics, truth and the impact of narrative research that go further than our earlier addresses to 'what is' and 'how to' questions.

Now, though, we are going to explore those questions about what narrative research is, by looking at a particular story.

B. What is narrative research?

Key new terms: *Narrative, narrative research, analysis of narratives versus narrative analysis, narrative inquiry.*

First, we will define some key terms in the narrative research field. The best way to do this, in a book about narrative research, is to start with a narrative. Below, we have quoted a story from a speech given by Vanessa Nakate, the influential young climate activist from Uganda. Nakate was speaking in 2022, on her appointment as a UNICEF Goodwill Ambassador, about her recent visit to northern Kenya. We refer to this narrative to demonstrate some of the salient features of contemporary narrative research, which addresses stories about issues from the highly personal to the global; takes in stories told in intimate surroundings and in international fora; and pays attention to the structure, content and context of stories.

> Vanessa Nakate: I met an 18-year-old mother named Dorcas, whose 20-month-old baby Micah was malnourished. Dorcas told me that she had not had enough food to feed Micah since he was born, and tried to explain the pain and stress of not being able to provide your child with something to eat.
> The drought means Dorcas has to travel so far to collect water that she has to sleep on the way before resuming her journey the next day.
> Thankfully, with support from UNICEF and their partners, Dorcas is able to visit a nutrition clinic where Micah can be assessed for malnutrition and receive lifesaving ready to use therapeutic food. She told me that without this support, baby Micah would not still be with us today.
> Climate activists often read about the impacts of climate change, and the statistics that show the scale of the crisis. But my visit to Kenya allowed me to learn the stories of the people, and the children, behind the statistics. Stories like Dorcas's and Micah's. (UNICEF, 2022)

By reading Nakate's narrative, we can explore some key aspects for narrative research.

First, what is a *narrative*? A broad, inclusive definition is that it is a set of signs. It might involve signs that are audible, as with music and speech – like Nakate's spoken narrative, broadcast live from a press conference and available later as a recording. The signs might be visible, as with film, sequences of gestures or written words – Nakate's narrative also appears in a YouTube video of her speaking and in a transcribed written version. A narrative set of signs could also be kinaesthetic, as with walking, dancing and other actions – for instance, Nakete's and our own physical engagements with, respectively, telling, and hearing or reading, her narrative.

For such signs to constitute a narrative, there needs to be movement between them. This movement may happen in time, across space and/or causally (Esin, 2017; Ryan, 2022). In a narrative, such symbolic movement is also not random; its order generates meaning. Because a narrative builds meaning in this way, rather than simply articulating one meaning after another, it provides *explanation* rather than just description. For instance, Nakate's narrative moves from Nakate's meeting with Dorcas, through Dorcas's own story of the difficulties, intensified by climate emergency, of feeding her child, back to Nakate's account of the UNICEF nutrition clinic and thence to the importance of stories themselves for mobilizing support for UNICEF's work. This narrative moves across time, developing knowledge as it goes.

Narratives also build particular, rather than general, explanations and knowledge. Because of this particularity, a narrative is not necessarily a 'theory', as we conventionally think of theory. It is tied to the specific phenomena it explains rather than being a general explanation of, for instance, political action or social change. Nakate herself emphasizes the importance of narratives' particularity, in contrast to general accounts of climate emergency, for instance.

In addition, because narratives build up explanations of psychological, social, cultural and political phenomena, there are likely to be social and historical limitations on where and when narratives can be understood and by whom. Nakate's previous story within the same speech, about another child in similar circumstances whom she met and who died before he could get adequate help, provided prior context that helped listeners and readers understand Dorcas's and Micah's story. But it might still be hard to understand their story without some knowledge of how climate emergency is intensifying food insecurity and child mortality in low- and middle-income countries. And citizens of these countries, who may have experience of climate emergency-related child deaths, may read the story differently than others.

Despite this variability in how stories are read, full, careful narratives, collectively generated and from multiple perspectives, can be the best kinds of explanation (Boonzaier et al., 2024; Namiba et al., 2023; Canham, 2023). Nakate's retelling of Dorcas's story explains, in a condensed and sophisticated way, the intersectionalities – the interconnected social structures of discrimination – between age, gender, food and water poverty, and climate emergency. A theoretical social science account of the same phenomenon would likely be less complex and less economical and might fail to convey the lived intersectionality that inhabits the story. Boonzaier (2019) and Phoenix (2023) have similarly shown the value of narrative research for understanding intersectionalities in their studies of, respectively, sex workers in South Africa and serial migrants in the UK.

There are many definitions of narrative that are more specific than the one we have given here. Such definitions may focus on narratives as making sense of temporality; developing or expressing personal identity; recording or witnessing the past; understanding mental states or emotions; having particular social effects; or demonstrating formal linguistic properties. They may contain more than one component and often overlap. Our definition here is very broad. You could think about what qualifications of our definition you might want to make as you read further in the book.

So far, we have used the terms 'story' and 'narrative' interchangeably. How is a story different from a narrative? Nakate declares that her account 'amplifies' the 'stories of the people, and the children, behind the statistics'. Some narrative researchers distinguish between recounted sequences of events, which they call 'stories', and organized, plotted, interpreted accounts of events, which are, for them, 'narratives'. From this perspective, Dorcas told a story about her child, while Nakate made a narrative out of that story when she 'amplified' the story within her speech. We are going to look at the story/narrative distinction in more detail in Chapter 2. For the moment, we can note that Nakate's speech could be said to create a dialogue with Dorcas's story by entraining it into a 'progress narrative', plotted to convey children's climate emergency-related starvation and UNICEF's mitigation of that starvation (Horton, 2019). And so, because of the narrative characteristics of Nakate's account, and because Nakate herself framed the account as having narrative qualities – as conveying both particularity and a broader significance through, as she put it, 'the stories of the people, and the children, behind the statistics' – her account seems like good material for narrative research.

Since, as we have seen, the signs making up narratives vary in type and occur in different media and modalities, *narrative research* involves working with narrative materials of diverse kinds. Sometimes, those materials already exist – for instance, if you are studying a computer game, a novel, a film or a speech of the kind you have just read. At other times, the narrative materials come into existence through the research process. In this second case, the researcher might ask their research participants to *produce* stories or narratives. These could be spoken life stories or photographic self-portraits or day-by-day journals of events. Alternatively, the researcher may generate material that will likely include narratives but without explicitly asking for them – for instance, by suggesting research participants write about their personal experiences or asking them to draw a family tree or encouraging them to talk at length about something that matters strongly to them.

Whether you find or produce the narrative material, the second aspect of narrative research involves analysing that material, trying to categorize or interpret it. This is *analysis of narratives*. You can analyse narratives without actually taking their narrative character into account – including quantitatively. Baele and colleagues, for instance (Baele et al., 2019), quantitatively map terms within the social media narratives of young men who are 'involuntarily celibate' or 'incel', and hostile to young women, to yield a 'world view' finding. Similarly, we could simply conduct a quantitative content analysis of words related to climate emergency – like 'children', 'Africa', 'food', 'water', 'poverty' and 'power' – in Nakate's Dorcas narrative and other UNICEF ambassador narratives. Or we could conduct a qualitative analysis, such as a reflexive thematic analysis (Braun and Clarke, 2021) of Nakate's narratives, without paying attention to the features that distinguish her narratives from descriptions. *Narrative analysis*, however, involves analysing the specifically narrative aspects of stories, not just analysing them in any way you think suitable. Most narrative researchers are keen to examine narratives *as* narratives; so we will be concentrating on narrative analysis, rather than analysis of narratives, in this book.

C. What do narrative researchers do?

Key new terms: *Narrative interests in truth and truths; narrative resource and 'theme', naturalism and constructionism; narrative focus on structure, content and context; reflexivity and ethics; programmatic and pragmatic narrative research.*

There are diverse reasons to be interested in narrative research. We will consider them in detail within Chapter 5's examination of the uses of narrative, but it's worth sketching them preliminarily here.

First, some researchers are interested in what narratives say about people and the world: that is, in narrative as what Kenneth Plummer (2019) has called a *resource*. In this case, researchers are concerned about the *truth* of narratives – their accurate representation of realities. When, as often happens, researchers address narratives that include psychic and social as well as physical realities, those researchers may argue that they are dealing with multiple narrative *truths*, some of which depend on the psychosocial, historical and political positions of their narrators (Andrews, 2014; Josselson and Hammack, 2021; Riessman, 2008). Researchers may also argue that single truths inevitably carry dangers of omission, error and inequity. The writer Chimamanda Adichie (2009) makes this point in her TED talk, 'The dangers of a single story', confronting essentializing, racist stories about 'Africa' such as those Nakate challenges.

Secondly, researchers' interest often centres on narratives as what Plummer (2019) described as *themes* in themselves. This interest leads researchers to analyse how narratives work, and how they affect people's understandings and actions in the world. In these cases, narrative researchers will be less concerned with the truth or truths of narratives, even if they think such truths exist.

Jane Elliott has described this dichotomy in narrative research interests as a division between *naturalism* (i.e. narrative as resource) and *constructionism* (i.e. narrative as theme). 'The naturalist view is that the social world is in some sense "out there", an external reality available to be observed and described by the researcher' (Elliott, 2005: 18), with language – including narratives – as the transparent window through which we access that reality. The constructionist approach explores how meaning is constructed in narratives in relation to available cultural, social and interpersonal resources (see also Esin, Fathi and Squire, 2013). Representations, including narratives, are, for this approach, the means by which we know of the world.

Vanessa Nakate, for instance, provides what is clearly a narrative resource: a truthful story about Dorcas's struggle to feed her child and the importance of the UNICEF therapeutic food intervention for the child's survival. The story does not refer to potential other important and sustaining contributions to that child's survival, such as family and community care and long-term food security. This incompleteness does not invalidate the story; it just suggests that a fuller narrative resource might encompass other truths too.

But Nakate's narrative is also a 'theme' in itself. How is it constructed? What is the *narrative structure*, grammar or syntax that makes it work? Structure is an important focus of narrative researchers' analysis. Adopting this focus, researchers might ask questions like: How does Nakate's narrative build Dorcas's story into her wider narrative of the UNICEF therapeutic food programme? And how does Dorcas's story fit into the speech as a whole – the broader narrative of the climate emergency's impacts on young people, especially those most affected in the majority world, and the absence of these key actors from climate activism, policy and politics? Nakate herself provides a guide to such structural analysis. She suggests that the narrative works by Dorcas's story standing in for a much larger whole – that is, by the rhetorical device of synecdoche – and by a contiguous association between Dorcas's story and the narrative Nakate herself tells to powerful audiences – that is, by metonymy. More generally, Dorcas's and Nakate's personal narratives claim a 'right to narrate', which is, Homi Bhabha (2010) has suggested, a necessary, though not sufficient, condition of cultural and social representation. As Nakate says of herself,

> In this new role, I commit to representing children everywhere – but especially those from the most affected areas.
> I will stand in for them where they don't have a seat yet at the table, and tell their stories to those who have the power to bring real change. (UNICEF, 2022)

Such concern with the structure or grammar of narratives, their linguistic organization, their plotting and genres is particularly strong in relation to written and media narratives, where it has a long history and strong current presence in literary and cultural studies and where it is often associated with *narratology*, various kinds of discourse analysis and semiotics (e.g. Bal, 1985; De Fina and Johnstone, 2015; Madisson and Ventsel, 2020).

Second, we might focus our analysis on the *narrative content* or meanings of a narrative – such as the personal, family, national and international histories, struggles and resistances that Nakate's narrative conveys. This analytic focus fits well with an interest in narrative as resource. An important aspect of such work is to distinguish it clearly from content or thematic analysis in general. Narrative thematic analysis focuses on themes that develop across narratives rather than just on themes that can be picked out from narratives (Hall, 2015; Ndlovu, 2012; Riessman, 2008).

Third, we might focus our analysis on *narrative context*: on how Nakate's narrative worked and what it did, both its performance and how its immediate audiences saw, heard and read it, and its place in the broader context of climate change and young people in the majority world. This analytic focus, which connects the immediate context of storytelling, with all its gaps, omissions, hesitations and incoherences, with the social context – from the microsocial interpersonal context of an immediate telling to the much broader sociocultural formations within which storytelling happens – could serve an interest in narrative as both theme and resource (Esin, 2017; Gubrium and Holstein, 2008; Ochs and Capps, 2001; Phoenix, 2013; Riessman, 2008). The immediate context of Nakate's narrative was that she was speaking as the first young African woman and climate change activist to be a UNICEF Goodwill Ambassador at a press conference to announce her appointment. This event had its own narrative conventions, within and against which her narrative was performed and had effects. It generated considerable international media coverage, and the speech retains online currency.

Within a larger socio-historical context, Nakete spoke as a young but long-time climate activist, dedicated to bringing neglected and excluded youth and majority-world perspectives into climate crisis policy and politics. She also spoke as someone who was notoriously, two years before, cropped out of a photo of young climate activists by an international press agency, leaving only white, minority-world activists in the frame – an aspect of context often mentioned in media accounts of her speech (Lakhani, 2022). We can thus trace many historical and present lines of intersectional storytelling, crossing hierarchized social categories (Boonzaier, 2019; Phoenix, 2022); broader discourses – structures of language and power – of colonialism and racism, ageism and climate change denialism; and recent shifts in material realities – in this case, the climate emergency-associated drought in northern Kenya and its drastic effects on child health. All of these provide context for Nakate's narrative.

Bruner (2002) explains how humans, as storytellers, are guided both by our own memories and by implicit cultural models of what 'selfhood' should be and how it should be narrated. This applies to narrative researchers themselves, who are also part of the research context. Their reflections on their involvement and the ethics of their research, considered in more detail throughout the book but especially in Chapter 1, Section D and Chapter 6, Section F, are also contextual activities. This aspect of 'contextual' analysis is, in part, institutionally regulated by ethical approval boards. But narrative researchers are particularly aware of the need to consider their work as an ethico-political process extending way beyond institutional ethical approval (Esin and Lounasmaa, 2020). Nakate's story is a public one, and research on such material does not require approval from academic or professional ethics committees. This does not mean that narrative researchers should analyse it without considering processual care, truth, respect and dignity. In this case, for instance, our own positioning as climate-concerned older white academics from the minority world inflects and limits our considerations of Nakate's story.

Verbal and other signs, cultural codes, and the discursive positioning of narrators, audiences and narrative researchers thus all interact within an open, always-shifting contextual matrix (Derrida, 1979) to perform and co-construct stories. And narrative researchers are increasingly attentive to how context happens, its complexities and the degree to which it – and they themselves – constitute the story.

These three structural, content and context focuses of narrative analysis are not mutually exclusive (Bengtsson and Andersen, 2020; Mishler, 1995). As indicated earlier, it is not possible to understand, for example, the content of Nakate's narrative without some sense of its wider context. Most narrative researchers who are interested in narrative content address narrative context as well. For example, Natasha Carver (2021), in her research about marriage and gender roles as narrated by UK Somali-origin women and men, works ethnographically and thematically and also provides a detailed structural and micro-contextual account of narrative processes.

In addition, there are many narrative research approaches to theory and methodology within and across these three categories, as well as approaches that cut across two or three of these. Some researchers call their own approach by a particular name and specify why they consider it the best. We could call this way of working *programmatic* narrative research. However, many researchers use more than one approach. They adopt what we might call a *pragmatic* research style, concentrating on what the research will do and for whom. They may choose theories, methodologies, data and modes of analysis that are not unique to a particular approach, or that come from different approaches, while also trying to ensure they take account of theoretical and methodological commonalities and differences between approaches.

We are going to address different theoretical and methodological approaches to narrative research in more detail later in this book. For now, we want to suggest that you try to keep the distinctions between different approaches in mind and to be conscious of possible contradictions. We hope that once you have familiarized yourself with narrative research through this overview, you will be able to include narrative research, or elements of it, in research projects you undertake, with a clear sense of why you are doing so and why you have chosen those specific elements.

D. Where do we find narratives?

Key new terms: *Spoken and interview narratives, recording, transcripts, written narratives, moving and still image narratives, media narratives, activity narratives, object narratives, emotional narratives, body narratives, paralinguistic narratives, sound narratives, small and big stories, top-down and bottom-up narrative analysis.*

From the approaches to narrative analysis and the definitions of narratives considered so far, you can see that narrative materials can be found across very different media and modalities. Perhaps the most obvious forms of narratives, for social researchers, are *spoken narratives*, very often obtained as *interview narratives*, alongside their *recordings* and *transcripts*, and *written narratives*. There is a lot of diversity even within these fairly straightforward categories. For instance, some narratives seem more fragmentary than others, particularly in their spoken versions, and might not 'count' as narratives for all researchers – although increasingly, apparently 'fragmented' narratives are, as we shall see later, becoming materials for narrative research (Hyvärinen et al., 2010; Ochs and Capps, 2001). Recordings may involve sound or audiovisual technologies. Decisions about how to transcribe audio and sometimes visual materials vary, and transcriptions themselves, therefore, constitute diverse kinds of narrative material. Written narratives come in many forms and are strongly affected by particular socio-historically shaped technologies and genres.

Beyond the words themselves, there are also a great many other symbols within and around spoken narratives to which narrative researchers are increasingly trying to pay attention. Researchers interested in linguistics and conversation analysis often include silence, voice pitch and timbre, and other paralinguistic elements such as laughs and sighs that accompany oral narratives. Increasingly, they use video so that they can also analyse eye, head, hand and body movements in their analyses (L. C. Hydén, 2013, 2018a). This material is especially good at conveying *emotional narratives* (Soundy, 2018), as we shall see when we consider the role of the body in narratives (Chapter 4, Section A). For some researchers, this kind of material, whose symbolic meanings are often quite mobile, is also the place to look for the *unconscious narratives* which appear within spoken or written material as subtextual, 'silent' stories, inviting debate about how they can be identified and interpreted (Freeman, 2012; Hollway and Jefferson, 2012; Wengraf, 2019).

Many narrative researchers are interested in how visual, auditory and physical materials work as narratives. However, there is debate over whether a still image, an object or a sequence of music can be said to be a narrative. Perhaps images and objects are simply distillations of or moments within narratives. A piece of music or a dance may have a narrative title; does it always constitute, temporally and sonically or physically, a narrative? An everyday photo or a keepsake on a mantelpiece may be part of someone's 'family story'; it may also be the catalyst for a broader interview narrative (Harrison, 2002; Bell, 2009; Luttrell, 2020). The case is clearer with moving or sequenced-image materials like comics, theatre, opera, film, television and internet texts. These materials have visual narrative progressions built into them and often support their image, object and physical narratives with words. We will consider these debates further when discussing visual and digital media narratives (Chapter 3, Sections B and C).

Some researchers have argued that symbolically structured patterns of activity – for instance, making art (Esin, 2017; getting, making and eating food (Sheringham and Taylor, 2022); taking care of people; shopping; collecting; getting, arranging and keeping your household possessions; and dying also have a narrative structure (Bal, 2004; Miller, 2021; Seale, 2004). Even walking around your everyday environment can have the attributes of a narrative (Fathi, 2023; O'Neil and Roberts, 2020). Buildings such as factories, shops, museums, temples, mosques and cathedrals are set up and used in ways that entrain people into a narrative progression through them (Ryan, 2022). Interest in these activity or process narratives (Esin and Squire, 2013; Squire, Esin and Burman, 2013) has led to increasing inclusion of ethnographic or observational and longitudinal elements within narrative research. For example, Wendy Luttrell's (2020) decades-long research with young people in a working-class eastern US city involved the young people making images of and talking about their lives in and outside their homes and schools. But the researcher also recorded her ethnographic observations of those settings, including the processes of image-making, and reflected on her own involvement with the project. All this material, together, formed the research narratives (see, similarly, Esin and Squire, 2013; Lounasmaa et al., 2020).

Narratives can also be said to extend into the phenomena that surround and support them. As we have seen, context is always an important part of narrative, since it is what enables narrative to be understood. Thus, personal narratives can be read as including the current and past social and cultural narratives within which they are situated. For instance, we can see the contextual matrix of Nakate's narrative as including her prior book (2021) outlining her path to climate activism as a young African woman; the speech's international policy context, particularly the preceding Glasgow COP26 climate change conference to which scandalously few

African delegates and climate activists were able to gain access; and more broadly, the failure of rich nations, by far most responsible for climate destruction, to provide loss and damage compensation for those middle and low-income countries most affected.

Developing this understanding of the multiple locations of narratives, many researchers have started to examine intertextual, hypertextual or transmedial narratives that include a number of different, linked narratives, in varieties of media, that can stretch across historical time and social situations. David Herman (2018, 2013), for instance, has described the 'storyworlds', the related, intersecting stories and background, accreted around alien invasion, in successive twentieth-century iterations of H. G. Wells's *War of the Worlds* story in book, radio, film and comic form, and around multi-species interactions in comic and graphic novels' verbal and visual narratives. Nakate's UNICEF speech can similarly, albeit with heavier consequence, be heard within the intersecting 'storyworlds' of international NGOs, climate activism and extractivist neocolonial racial capitalism.

We have spent some time considering where we might look for narratives. But where we think narratives are largely depends on what we think they are and how we think they should be studied. Researchers who address narrative as 'small stories' told during everyday interactions, for instance (Georgakopoulou, 2022), are not going to be very interested in extensive interview narratives, which appear in non-everyday contexts. Such researchers may, however, attend to diverse media where such everyday narratives occur, such as phone texts and social media videos. Researchers interested in narrative as 'big stories', for instance, extended and reflected upon individual life narratives, may not be too concerned about stories told in popular media, even if some aspects of these are similar to the material they are studying (Freeman, 2015).

At the same time, research materials themselves importantly shape what we think narrative is. Most narrative researchers aim to be respectful of their material rather than approaching it with a set idea of what counts as narrative. That leads to interaction between *top-down*, deductive approaches to narrative research, drawing on existing definitions of narrative; and *bottom-up*, inductive research approaches, responsive to material of different kinds. This 'interaction' can amount to an undoing of the inductive and deductive categories themselves. It means that our sense of where narratives occur, routes to understanding them, and therefore, what narrative research is, are fluid, and that interconnections and overlaps between narrative and other materials, narrative research and other forms of research, are ubiquitous.

Such diversity may be the future of narrative research. What were its beginnings?

E. Where does narrative research come from?

Key new terms: *Event narrative, structural linguistics, poststructuralism, postmodernism, positioning, polysemy, subjectivities, the unconscious, intertextuality, transmediality, anti-positivism, humanism, phenomenology, narrative inquiry, decoloniality, cognitvism, theory-method, narrative as theory.*

The origins of narrative research are complex. This section reviews some of its historical beginnings, clustering them in broad-brush categories to help us think about the shape of the contemporary field.

Narrative research is often said to originate with 1920s Russian formalist linguistic analyses of stories – for instance, Vladimir Propp's categorization of the functions served by narrative units within fairy tales. Propp counted thirty-one functions, following a 'Once upon a time' opening, and claimed they occurred in an invariant order. This tradition is hard to tie to contemporary narrative social research because it was concerned much more with narratives as themes than with narratives' content or their social functioning – that is, with narratives as resources (see Section C). However, the tradition influenced later structurally oriented psycholinguistic and sociolinguistic analyses of the functional 'grammar' of spoken stories. These analyses similarly treated narratives as themes within research.

In particular, the formalist tradition contributed to the work of William Labov, who described what he claimed to be the universal category of *event narratives* – spoken first-person narratives about past events that happened to the teller. Such narratives, Labov said, are distinguished by (a) 'complicating action' clauses that follow each other in time and (b) 'evaluative' material that makes sense of these happenings, telling you why the narrative matters (Labov, 1997; Labov, 1972; Labov and Waletsky, 1967; Patterson, 2013). The first part of Vanessa Nakate's narrative, in which she first 'met' Dorcas, who then 'told' her something, and afterwards 'explained' more about the situation, is an event narrative. It features narrative clauses where progression happens in time; Dorcas could not explain the issue to Nakate before she met her, for example. This is a skilful, condensed narrative. It does not require Nakate to evaluate it, because the evaluation – the importance of the story – is already conveyed within the complicating action, when Dorcas says she has never had enough food for her child and then gives an account of the 'pain and stress' that that produces.

In the next two sentences, Nakate departs from event narrative structure by providing her own account of other information that Dorcas gave her: about desertification leading to much longer trips for water and the UNICEF clinic allowing her to keep her child alive and healthy. This material also acts as evaluation. The resolution to the story, in Labov's terms, lies in Dorcas's clinic visit and Micah's survival. Nakate then provides what Labov would call a narrative coda, a link to what comes after the story, when she says, 'My visit to Kenya allowed me to learn the stories of the people, and the children, behind the statistics. Stories like Dorcas's and Micah's.'

For Labov, other kinds of speech, and narratives in other media, do not belong to this fundamental human communication category of event narrative. But, of course, people work with much larger and more variable definitions of narratives than those Labov used. 'Event narratives', for instance, are not everyone's preferred way of narrating. Such preferences may be gender- and culture-specific. Moreover, narratives about events that happened many times, narratives about what could happen in the future and narratives about what happened to other people are part of our story repertoires, even though they do not fall within Labov's definition. Nakate could have told a powerful story about Dorcas even if she had not met her, for example. In addition, 'event narratives' are very hard to separate from the material around them. Nakate's 'Dorcas' narrative is also prefaced by a related story about another child who died. The 'Dorcas' event narrative, therefore, does not stand alone, as, in Labov's account, it should, but relates crucially to material that came before it (Patterson, 2013).

Despite these issues, the Labovian framework is still used, albeit modified, to analyse some kinds of narratives and as a starting point for researchers who follow up their event narrative analysis with other kinds of narrative analysis (Bell, 2009; Yardley et al., 2020).

Somewhat later than the Russian formalists, structuralist linguistics, as developed by Saussure, Barthes, Levi-Strauss, Todorov and Genette, analysed narratives as sets of symbols with interdependent and mobile relationships to each other rather than as sets of symbols with straightforwardly available one-to-one meanings (see, e.g. Barthes, 1977; Todorov, 1990). This work, while interested in narrative structure, is also concerned with context – the symbolic contexts within which narratives accrete and communicate meaning. Many narrative researchers within the social sciences still draw on such work and thus maintain a focus on the language of narratives. Taking this approach, we might, for instance, look at how Nakate's speech names Dorcas and Micah, though other people Nakate met are not named. While NGO narratives often use naming to humanize suffering and perhaps also connote verifiability, its function here is different. Within a speech about the limited power of young Africans in the climate crisis, the names of Dorcas and Micah, alongside the narrative of Nakate herself, work through the 'right to narrate' (Bhabha, 2010) to assert agency and to challenge those who, as Nakate says, 'have the power to bring real change'.

Later *poststructuralist* and *postmodernist* intellectual movements took these arguments about the relationality of signs further to emphasize that symbol systems do not exist independently. Their characteristics of interconnection and fluid meanings also appear within the subjectivities that make and are made by them and across all of the broader social and cultural contexts within which subjects live. These ideas were influential first within humanities disciplines, shaping theorizations of narrative in, for instance, literature, cultural studies and history. However, such ideas also strongly affected social sciences (e.g. Gergen, 1991; Henriques et al., 1984/1998). This happened both at the level of 'small story' analysis, where narrative social research is now often related to conversation and discourse analysis (e.g. Bamberg, 2006; Georgakopoulou, 2007), and within work on larger life stories, which frequently draws on contemporary literary, cultural and social theory (Andrews,

2014; Bradbury, 2019; Canham, 2023; Davis, 2017; Meretoja and Freeman, 2023; Peterson, 2019).

In examining the Dorcas narrative, for example, an analysis drawing on these approaches might look at normative NGO narratives, which tend to deploy personal stories illustratively and to mobilize affect (Wells, 2013). It might then read Dorcas's story, and its deployment by Nakate, as counteracting that NGO narrative, as well as speaking back to stories of African non-subjecthood and of climate change denial. This is something the story achieves by foregrounding Dorcas's strength – and thence, the strength of many other young women in similar situations – and her clear explanation of the climate emergency's effects.

This kind of narrative analysis is interested in small- and large-scale narrative contexts. It examines the contextual *positionings* of narrators, narratives and audiences and how those positionings are constituted by discourses of power and knowledge. Such work often also operates with a constructionist view of how narratives work to make subjects (e.g. Esin et al., 2013; Phoenix, 2013; Bjorninen et al., 2020). It might, for instance, ask how Nakate's 'Dorcas' story is positioned within an assemblage of political, policy, cultural and activist narratives around climate change, youth, aid, and 'Africa'; and how it both calls on and constitutes certain kinds of subjects as its audiences. Nakate, the 'I' who is speaking, a UNICEF Global Ambassador – a category containing no other young African or climate activist – positions herself as a storyteller for climate emergency-affected youth. The narrative also expresses the positionality of Dorcas as a parent striving, as any parent would, to keep her child alive and as a theorist of climate change. And there is an implied audience for this speech, positioned as interested in UNICEF, climate emergency, youth, women and/or the majority world.

A number of other concepts connected with poststructuralism and postmodernism inflect contemporary narrative work. Researchers generally understand narrative language as having multiple meanings or being *polysemic*. They look for multiple *subjectivities* in play in narratives (Boonzaier, 2019; Riessman, 2008). They think of past, present and future as co-present in narratives (Freeman, 2009; Brockmeier, 2015). They may be interested in the inexpressible or incomprehensible *unconscious* elements of narratives and their psychoanalytic meanings (Hollway and Jefferson, 2012; Wengraf,

2019). They explore the *intertextualities* and *transmodality* of different forms of narratives spoken, imaged, acted out in our lives, lived in bodily experiences, broadcast in popular media and performed by institutions (Davis, 2017; Harrison, 2002; Herman 2018; L. C. Hydén, 2018a, 2013; Phoenix, 2022; Ryan, 2022). Many of the conceptual moves sketched above have been fruitful for thinking about narrative, narrators and audiences. However, there are some general challenges arising from poststructural and postmodern approaches. It is questionable whether narratives can adequately be understood socially, historically or politically within these very specific conceptual traditions (Abdi, 2023; Boonzaier, 2019; Canham, 2023). Within this conceptual framework, how usefully can we analyse narratives' powers, resistances and effects? These are questions we will return to very soon, in Section F.

Some narrative social research has taken a 'cognitive' turn, which hopes to resolve many of the questions raised so far about what narrative is, how it works and what it does. Such cognitive work has developed mainly among researchers working with literary and other media texts. They draw on cognitive psychology and sometimes psychologically framed models of neurology to ground narrative in underlying cognitive, neurological and other biological processes (Fludernik, 2010; Hatavara et al., 2016; Herman, 2018; see also Hutto and Myin, 2017; Ryan, 2022). This approach recalls prior linguistic work on narrative, for instance, that of Labov and Waletsky (1967) and Gee (1991), in treating narrative language as relatively transparent and narrative as a universal sense-making device tied into other cognitive and social abilities. Cognitivism thus offers a relatively universalized understanding of what narrative is, its underpinnings and its significance. But it has been criticized for lack of rigour in 'importing' concepts, being cognitively and neurologically reductionist and equating cognition with language. It sometimes also adopts poorly empirically supported psychological and neurological models.

Narrative research also has a parallel *humanist* history, associated with early-twentieth-century studies of the fine grain of people's lives, such as Thomas and Znaniecki's *The Polish Peasant in Europe and America* (1918–20), and with post-war western social sciences' *anti-positivism*, a response to the failures of broad-brush 'positivist' empirical and theoretical understandings of society (Stanley, 1995), as in Wright Mills's *Sociological Imagination* (1959). At the same time, humanism became more significant in western psychology, both clinically and academically, opposing the reduction of subjectivity to dependent variables measurable in experiments or to unconscious factors knowable only by an inducted psychoanalytic elite. Late-twentieth-century humanist psychology itself included a narrative strand (Polkinghorne, 1988; Sarbin, 1986), viewing lives as actively storied, linking narration to agency. The work within this tradition most quoted by narrative researchers is probably the philosopher Ricoeur's (1984) phenomenological writing on narratives as making human sense of time and the psychologist Bruner's (1990) framing of narratives as 'stories we live by'. Generally, such work concentrates on narrative as resource – on the meaningful content of stories, more than on their structure and contexts. Humanist-psychological narrative research also exhibited a tendency to draw on 1950s US literary critic Northrop Frye's Aristotelian-influenced account of narrative genres of comedy, tragedy, romance and irony as human universals, at the same time as literary theory was questioning the validity of both literary categorization and categories shaped by Eurocentrism.

F. Narrative research today: Social justice and re-humanization

Contemporary narrative research often draws on the meaning-oriented humanist narrative research tradition alongside the more structure- and context-oriented 'poststructural' and 'postmodern' traditions. The resultant narrative endeavour questions the culturally and politically specific and discriminatory assumptions attending western 'Enlightenment' concepts of the 'human' (Foucault, 1994; Mbembe, 2015) and 'experience' (Scott, 1992) and the epistemic power that such western framings of narrative give to minority-world narrators and researchers. Such work questions characterizations of human experience and narrative itself as universal, unchanging and progressive (Henriques et al., 1984/19898).

For instance, Plummer's (2019) 'critical humanist' narrative approach is informed by Foucault's ideas about the constructed nature of human experience and the power relations that inhere in narratives. This awareness puts into question humanist valuations of narratives as unproblematic foundations of progressive personal and social change. 'Narrative inquiry' approaches adopt a pragmatic account of 'experience', as what people do (Dewey, 1892) rather than as a solely internal phenomenon. From this perspective, narratives of experience are a kind of 'testing' of the world – as the word 'experience''s origin in *experientia*, the Latin for 'test' or 'experiment', suggests. In narrative inquiry, narratives operate as 'experience' themselves. Researchers explore narratives alongside their research participants while recognizing the different positions and powers that inflect that relationship. For example, Trudy Cardinal and colleagues have developed a narrative inquiry about teaching curricula and assessments' relation to Canadian Aboriginal and non-Aboriginal people and ways of thinking. It involves autobiographical work conducted by the researchers alongside other teachers, students of all ages and parents (Cardinal, Murphy and Huber, 2019; see also Clandinin and Connelly, 2004; Clandinin et al., 2018). And Muna Abdi (2023) developed a 'community contract' that worked alongside the institutional consent process, recognizing the disempowering aspects of that process in itself. That community contract, again based on relationality rather than rights and responsibilities, enabled participants to hold researchers to account in relation to principles agreed before and during the research.

One effect of these co-articulations of context, ethics and politics within contemporary narrative research is to foreground participants' own research roles. This participant-centring may lead to various levels of participant involvement in the research. Drawing on related approaches within Critical Participatory Action Research, narrative researchers may enable participants' co-research alongside them, frequently with explicit social change aims (Del Tufo et al., 2021; Lyndon and Edwards, 2022; Fine and Torre, 2021). Or participation can become full ownership, as with Angelina Namiba's and her colleagues' collection of stories mapping the powerful and creative African response to HIV in the UK, *Our Stories Told by Us*. Of these 'stories we don't usually read about', the editors say, 'it was pivotal for Africans living with HIV to lead this project and to tell our own stories in our own words' (Namiba et al., 2023: 13).

We have already seen how narratives operate as a kind of theory in the case of Dorcas and Vanessa Nakate. These contemporary forms of narrative research also frequently position participants' narratives not just as 'data' or 'material' but as theory in themselves (Abdi, 2023; Boonzaier et al., 2024; Carver, 2021; Namiba et al., 2023). For instance, Hugo Canham (2023: 5) in *Riotous Deathscapes* gives a far-reaching account of the subjectivities, geographies and histories of Mpondo people, whose land lies in the coastal region of South Africa's Eastern Cape. He describes his 'transcription' of their bodily and worldly lives as 'Mpondo theory'.

Relatedly, as we can see in Cardinal and colleagues' work, narrative research often mobilizes distinct and different epistemologies that originate from the research participants – in this case, from indigenous approaches that ask ethico-political rather than technical questions about method: 'How am I fulfilling my role in this relationship (with all elements of the world)? What are my obligations in this relationship?' (Wilson, 1977 cited in Cardinal, Murphy and Huber, 2019: 83).

A further effect of bringing context, ethics and politics together in current narrative research is to increase researchers' engagement with the broader politics of their work. Researchers are challenging what Boonzaier (2019: 468, citing Tuck and Wayne Yang, 2014) calls out as social research 'perpetuating marginalisation, doing little more than perpetuating, repackaging and recirculating stories of pain, oppression and damage'. Content-based narrative research may normalize such damage by simply foregrounding it; small-scale structural narrative analyses can perform a similar normalization by bracketing off disenfranchisements. In response, many narrative researchers and practitioners now work with narratives as political forces that gather people together and potentiate action (Plummer, 2019) and that are themselves forms of political action when they involve, for instance, witnessing trauma, forced migration and state violence. The *Our Stories Told by Us* authors are deliberately changing the narratives – and, in the process, the practices – around people from African backgrounds and HIV in the UK. Del Tufo and colleagues' (2021) work, while archiving narratives of the 1960s US civil rights struggle, creates a dialogue for the present and the future between activists in that struggle and youth. For Cardinal and colleagues (2019), situating their work within histories of settler colonialism's educational violence against indigenous people, narrative research becomes a pedagogy to transform pedagogy itself (see also Lykes, 2021; Del Tufo et al., 2021; Bradbury, 2019; Esin and Lounasmaa, 2020).

Contemporary narrative research's extensive engagement with social justice often goes along with challenges to western ontological and epistemological conventions. First, although such research involves varying perspectives and multiple stories, it is not operating as a relativistic exploration of multiple truths but rather, as we suggested in Section C of this chapter, building larger truths – a fuller, though necessarily incomplete, knowledge (also see Chapter 6, Section G).

Second, current narrative research's attention to its sociopolitical positioning means questioning not just what conventional western concepts of epistemology and ontology involve but also those concepts' separation, necessity and history. When you start doing social research, you are often encouraged to position your work ontologically, in terms of where you think existence or being lies and what it consists of; and epistemologically, in terms of where you think knowledge can be found and how it is made. Frequently, narrative researchers position their work very equivocally – as ontologically realist, but in a qualified way, and as epistemologically somewhere between empiricism and constructionism. Such equivocations also start to undo the historically and socially particular conceptual divide between ontology and epistemology. Researchers like Ronelle Carolissen and Peace Kiguwa (2018), in their work on students' verbal and visual narratives of citizenship, belonging and alienation in (mainly) South African universities, have superseded these traditional categories, arguing that narrative research should be treated as a 'theory-method' since it both views narratives, their effects and production as central to people's lives and takes narratives, their effects and production as the material for its knowledge. Similarly, Canham (2023: 5) has described his 'meditation and portrait of black life lived in the rural reserve' by Mpondo people as a 'theory-method of being' (see also Abdi, 2023).

As many narrative and other researchers have pointed out, theory and method, ontology and epistemology are not divisible in indigenous ways of knowing (Cardinal, Murphy and Huber, 2019; Eagle Heart, n.d.; Tuhiwai Smith, 1999). Splitting the two is a kind of epistemic violence, echoing that performed by concepts of the 'human' and 'experience'. The split constitutes colonized, enslaved, racialized and otherwise excluded others as the 'field', the objects of knowledge. This matter from which theory can be extracted, these data to be 'mined', are set against knowers and knowledge (Ndlovu-Gatsheni, 2015; Nhemachena et al., 2016; Ratele, 2019; Spivak, 1988).

Such epistemic oppression may appear in the concepts and ownership of narrative and narrative research, which majority-world narrative researchers now challenge. Sarah Eagle Heart (n.d.) insists that non-linear, relational indigenous storytelling needs to be recognized, not pathologized, exoticized or undervalued in comparison with a dominant, normalizing account of linear narratives emanating from distinct individual subjects:

> Why should I change the way that I think or talk? There has to be an acceptance of that circular storytelling, of sharing things in a way that is nonlinear. There has to be an acceptance of it, and the patience to stretch yourself beyond a Western structure and be able to say, 'Okay, I can take in this knowledge, and in a way that is more organic.' (Eagle Heart, n.d.)

And as herself the researcher of her own story, Bakita Kasadha in *Our Stories Told by Us* advises, 'Tell your story on your own terms. You don't need to cut yourself wide open to share it' (Namiba et al., 2023: 82–3).

We could understand these increasing concerns with social justice within narrative research in terms of researchers' increasing awareness of much older, broader and more powerful forms of narrative research and practice. Plummer (2019) points out that popular narrative practices have always both critically challenged dominant power relations and generated their own alternative framings of sociality. This association between narration and political action appears in the importance of personal speech and writing in majority-world anti-colonial struggles for and after independence (Beverley, 2004; Biko, 2002; Chungara, 1978; Selbin, 2010) and in anti-slavery, working-class, feminist, lesbian and gay rights and civil rights struggles (Dadzie et al., 2018; Gobodo-Madikizela, 2003; Hull et al., 2015; Jolly, 2019; Moraga, 2015; Namiba et al., 2023; Personal Narratives Group, 1989; Plummer, 1995; Polletta, 2006).

Narrative engagements are not all, of course, directed at progressive social change. Many are regressive or conservative;

some eschew politics for explanation or entertainment. However, current narrative social research has learned much of its current politics from narratives' own progressive engagements. An important continuation of narratives' progressive histories lies in the anti-colonial and decolonial, as well as the anti-racist, feminist, and other social justice commitments of contemporary narrative research. Abdi's (2023) extended 'community' ethics contract was formulated according to an explicit commitment to work outside of colonial framings and appropriations of knowledge. Boonzaier notes that decolonial commitments work against dominant knowledge productions' 'dehumanizing' effects. Considering how narrative criminology addresses sex work, for instance, she says, 'a decolonial approach (within narrative research) is important because it allows us to see the historical roots of the contemporary oppressions faced by poor women sex workers, that might otherwise be erased' (2019: 470).

The political effects of narratives and narrative research in the pursuit of social justice are often powerful, as some of the above examples have suggested (see later, especially Chapter 4 and Chapter 6). But narratives' political effects are also limited. Narrative research does not 'give voice' to oppressed, let alone excluded people. It is more that people lend their voices to research (Portelli, 2010) that can, as Nakate says of her own speech, 'amplify' those voices. The consequences are not always predictable or wanted; and narrative researchers may overwhelm participant voices with their own.

As well, narratives do not make change by themselves, and they frequently have only limited impact. Nakate's story challenges dominant donor narratives which, despite commitments to international human rights, were paying little attention to the interactions between climate emergency, food insecurity and child mortality. But Nakate's narrative is operating alongside weakened international rights narratives and largely performative minority-world narratives of climate action. Unsurprisingly, positional narratives like Nakate's have not yet brought about sufficient food relief for children in northern Kenya, let alone adequate 'loss and damage' funds for desertified regions.

There is an alternative narrative approach: to generate or amplify stories that are relational, empathetic and human, creating a kind of alter-politics (Hage, 2015), as indeed Eagle Heart (n.d.) and the

Our Stories Told by Us writers (Namiba et al., 2023) are doing. Nakate, too, told a story that went beyond criticism, enabling audiences to recognize and identify with Dorcas as a young woman, a mother and a parent, generating solidarity (Wells, 2013). However, such stories may be ignored or reified into emblematic but purely personal stories. In the worst cases, such narratives are used to weaponize empathy for political purposes, including war violence (Fernandes, 2017).

Should we consider narratives, and narrative research too, as politically useful projects when they are so limited in their effects? This an ongoing debate within narrative research. Later on, we return to the issue of what narrative research may achieve, both in terms of what the research itself does and in relation to the participants who lend their stories to the research (Chapter 5, Sections A, B and D; Chapter 6, Sections D–G).

In the next chapter, we provide a sample of contemporary arguments within the narrative field that build on the discussions above. To do this, we describe five current narrative research debates, which you will often encounter when reading and doing narrative research.

CHAPTER 2

What's the story? Five contemporary issues in narrative research

One of narrative research's most attractive features is that, as we saw in the first chapter, it is very diverse in its antecedents, its present theoretical and methodological possibilities and its constant evolutions. Consequently, many aspects of it are up for debate. In this chapter, we are going to give you a taste of some contemporary debates in narrative research before going on, in the next two chapters, to provide snapshots of narrative research in some of its key contemporary fields.

The first debate, about whether an accurate or useful distinction can be made between stories and narratives, might seem the simplest. However, as you will see, this debate, like those that follow, raises important broader issues that you may need to take into account when you are thinking about narrative research.

A. Is a narrative different from a story – and if not, why not? Stories, narratives, dialogue and co-construction

Key new terms: *fabula, syuzhet, dialogic narratives, co-constructed narratives.*

So far, although we mentioned early on the distinction researchers make between 'story' and 'narrative', we have been treating them as if they are the same thing. We will continue to use these terms interchangeably in the rest of this book. We need to explain why we are doing this because, as mentioned in Chapter 1, some narrative researchers make a distinction between 'stories' as sequences of events and the discursive organization of events into 'narratives'. The Russian formalist linguists of the 1920s insisted on this distinction between story or *fabula* and narrative or *syuzhet*. Using these terms, Dorcas's story about her efforts to feed Micah was a *fabula* and Vanessa Nakate then constructed a *syuzhet* out of it. The *fabula–syuzhet* distinction could then be seen as a useful way of distinguishing Dorcas's story – a highly specific, not really plotted account of events – from Nakate's retelling of it in a narrative, which progresses from Dorcas's own experiences to a more general account. 'Story' is, in this account, lower level, highly idiosyncratic and of less interest.

But in fact, Dorcas's 'story' is not merely a recounting of events but a complex 'narrative' condensation of them. Indeed, even the most spontaneous, rushed recountings of events, the most apparently obvious examples of 'story' or *fabula*, could be said to have the 'narrative' organization of *syuzhet* built into them. We live and speak in cultures characterized by narrative repertoires. When we tell the story of a sequence of events, it is inevitably narrativized, inflected by those repertoires, even if it seems like an immediate, individual and incomplete account.

What about material that seems to fall into the 'narrative' category of *syuzhet*? This apparently higher-order category can, conversely, itself be read as a 'story'. Nakate's 'narrative', for example, is also a 'story' told at a particular moment in an NGO campaign. And we always tell narratives to audiences, even if those audiences are only imagined. This interactivity, again, skews 'narrative' towards storying. Nakate addressed a UNICEF audience; her narrative is also in a kind of conversation with other stories told within the UNICEF 'family', as it's called here. As well, her narrative speaks to broader media audiences and to fellow youth climate activists, especially in Africa. Perhaps Nakate is, too, speaking to an African – and planetary – future audience. And she may, more personally, be holding in mind the women and children she met as she speaks. Narratives are, therefore, always dialogic (Bakhtin, 1982; Moen,

2006), involving ongoing exchanges between narrators and their audiences. This dialogic character makes them more particular, idiosyncratic and story-like than the notion of 'narratives' as plotted and ordered suggests.

Moreover Nakate's narrative is inflected variously by the media in which it appears. In its spoken version, it is constructed not just from the words we have been analysing but auditorially from the pitch, loudness, pauses, breaths and amplification for the physical audience. The narrative also appears in a pre-written version, identical to the post-speech transcript, and in Nakate's in-person, broadcast and recorded visual image. This *fabula*-like media particularity again undermines the speech as *syuzhet*.

Co-construction by narrators, audiences and media is, therefore, characteristic of all narratives. These co-constructed, contextual, 'story'- or *fabula*-related features of narratives cut across the 'narrative' organization of a *syuzhet*. And such factors could be argued to be just as much present in narrative materials as are the *syuzhet*-like 'narrative' elements of order and progression.

Because of these ambiguities, many narrative researchers suggest that the story/narrative, *fabula/syuzhet* distinction often breaks down, institutes an oppressive hierarchy valorizing *syuzhet* over *fabula* and is not very helpful (Culler, 2002; Derrida, 1979). We will, therefore, not be using the distinction any further in this book, although you will find it used within some contemporary narrative research.

Having put aside the distinction between 'narrative' and 'story' for the purposes of this book, let us look at another feature often said to define narratives: the coherence of 'good' narratives as against the incoherence of 'bad' or 'failed' narratives. This distinction is also being rewritten in contemporary narrative research (Hyvärinen et al., 2010).

B. Are all narratives, or all 'good' narratives, coherent?

Key new terms: *Coherence, foreshadowing, backshadowing, sideshadowing, conversational storytelling, supported storytelling.*

In Western literary narrative theory, there is a long tradition of stressing the *coherence* of stories. Such theory was, to a large degree, based on the study of European written texts, in particular, nineteenth-century novels, for instance, those of Balzac and Tolstoy. These written texts were often organized around a number of characters moving and acting in well-defined places and were temporally well ordered. This resulted in the idea that stories could be conceived of as if they form a unitary package of temporal linearity, thematic unity or completeness in terms of story characters. As well, coherence has been and remains an important criterion of narrative adequacy or success in many varieties of therapy that address narratives and in the work of many humanist-oriented narrative psychologists and social researchers (e.g. McAdams, 2021).

However, the idea of stories as inherently coherent was already questioned by literary modernists like Virginia Woolf and James Joyce, who radically undermined the assumed coherence of time and space, letting the characters define both time and space subjectively. It was also more broadly questioned by postmodern theorists for whom both character and text became problematic categories, with characters' subjectivities no longer privileged and literary texts seen as occurring intertextually across many social and cultural texts (Culler, 2002; Spivak, 1988).

The idea of temporal coherence in narratives, specifically, has been questioned by literary theorists like Gary Saul Morson (1994) and Michael André Bernstein (1994), who both have pointed out that narratives routinely play with multiple options. Consequently, they have suggested terms like *sideshadowing*, *foreshadowing* and *backshadowing* as ways of displacing the idea of temporal linearity. Their idea is that the narration lets events cast their shadows over the narrator's present. Shadows of time can come from the front, letting future events cast over characters (foreshadowing); from the back (backshadowing), understanding in retrospect how an event might have been foreseen; or from the side (sideshadowing), pointing to alternative courses of events and possibilities. Vanessa Nakete's Dorcas story, for example, started life as a written text and so has some affinities, in its structures of coherence, with other written narratives. It backshadows the present by beginning in the recent past, with Dorcas's own story and the events that led to it, but is textually surrounded by insistent descriptions of that present. At the speech's end, the immediate future effects of Nakate's amplifying voice are a foreshadowing marker for the only slightly less immediate future effects of the climate emergency. And throughout, as frequently happens in climate emergency narratives, the imperatives uttered – what we or they must do – sideshadow the alternative story endings with whose possibilities we – some more than others – are intimately living.

The idea of coherence becomes even more problematic in the study of *conversational stories*, that is, stories people tell in everyday situations. Researchers studying conversational storytelling like Elinor Ochs and Lisa Capps have pointed out that many conversational narratives are incomplete and only get completed in and through the interaction between the participants in the storytelling event (Ochs and Capps, 2001). This is, for instance, typically the case when parents tell stories together with children. As Peggy Miller has shown, parents often *support* children's storytelling by posing questions and suggestions, in this way producing a story that adheres to the classical norms of coherence (Miller and Sperry, 1988).

A similar production of coherence can happen for people with certain kinds of brain injuries or people suffering from, for instance, Alzheimer's disease. People with these conditions often have severe problems telling 'coherent' stories: they may jump between different points of time in the story or skip certain events without helping the listener; or they may tell the story or part of the story over and over again. In medical terms, these persons produce stories that are incoherent (L. C. Hydén and Antelius, 2011). At the same time, research shows that if someone supports the storytelling of the person with the disability, a story that is experienced by the listener as more coherent will often be produced. This indicates the importance of understanding storytellers not as isolated individuals but as participants co-constructing stories with others (L. C. Hydén, 2018a). Narrative researchers have argued that 'coherence' is a category that is not necessary or sufficient to define narratives or account for their effects (Hyvärinen et al., 2010). Indeed, we can see that coherence and incoherence do not exist as properties of stories or storytellers. They are present in the interactional telling and understanding of stories. Narrative coherence can, therefore, better be thought of as something storytellers and listeners can use as a resource in composing and telling a story, rather than as an inherent quality of stories.

The chapter's next section moves on to consider what is now recognized as the centrality of such interactions for narrative research.

C. Narrative, translation and multilinguality

Key new terms: *Translation, multilinguality.*

At times, we see it suggested that narratives and stories have a universal character and can hence provide access to experiences and meanings across linguistic and cultural barriers. In Chapter 1, for instance, many of the approaches we mentioned in psycholinguistic, cognitive and humanist narrative social research, as well as some literary narratological traditions, often operate with this assumption. Indeed, oral storytelling traditions in many cultural contexts would suggest that stories carry meaning in all the different contexts where they are produced. Here, however, we would disagree with those who suggest that this meaning can be universally accessed and interpreted using structural or content analytic tools.

There are several levels of translation that we must consider before we can begin to make sense of narratives that have emerged in linguistic and cultural settings different from ours and not of Eurocentric origins. First, we need to pay attention to the practical issues of languages. Riessman (2008) used an interpreter when conducting narrative interviews with Indian women but noted that this bears epistemological implications for the research. Brannlund et al. (2013) explore the challenges of translation as they affect different stages of the research process: formulation of research questions and protocols in such a way that they make sense in the research context and conducting field research and analysis.

Narratives are especially sensitive when it comes to translating them, as they are so essential to our identities and self-making. As narrative researchers, we are responsible for the careful recreation of participants' stories and identities in a new vernacular, and as Baker (2006) notes, we do this recreation through the lens of our own experiences (see also Temple and Kortega, 2009).

There are also times when translation and particular language policies are (mis)used deliberately to advance political goals and, as mentioned in the previous chapter, to weaponize empathy: Fernandes (2017) shows how storytelling and writing programme with Afghani women provided Western audiences with what looks like an authentic voice but what was deliberately constructed through narrative models and language to support US foreign policy goals in Afghanistan. In addition to the words and phrases, we are always translating cultural context and conventions.

The larger question of the hegemony of the English language in research and academic publication cannot be resolved merely by resolving technical questions with translation. Anzaldúa (1987), Spivak (2012), Ngũgĩ (1986) and many more have for decades questioned the requirement of existing through English or other colonial languages. As Patel and Spivy (2020, n.p.) remind us, a 'good' translation in this context is 'often defined according to how appealing it is to an imagined demographic of Anglophone readers'. Ngũgĩ suggests that meaning can only be communicated in the native tongue and that it is not the job of the African writer to make the story accessible to 'enrich other tongues'. Furthermore, he suggests that a technical translation can never be done, as the 'magical power of language' is created through riddles, proverbs, musically arranged words, images and symbols (1986: 8, 11). For Anzaldúa (1987), the trouble with translation is that it misses the point of multilingual identities and lives. Being forced to tell oneself in just one language and to modify that language into acceptable structures and patterns betrays the experience of living a multilingual and multicultural life.

A great deal of educational and artistic narratively based work creates models for multilingual storytelling, which engages critically with power relations in language use and translation. For example, the artist and researcher Sonia Quintero (https://soniaquintero.co.uk; Lounasmaa et al., 2024) embraces multilingual poetry writing as part of their community building and research practice in East London. When we do translate, we should use translation 'as an intimate listening exercise' (Patel and Spivey, 2020, n.p.). In addition to paying attention to language choices, publication and translation practices, the use of multimodality in narrative research (Esin and Lounasmaa, 2020), including images, sounds and paralanguage, may provide tools for thinking critically about narratives and language. We discuss these issues further in Chapter 3.

D. Does narrative research always involve reflexivity?

Key new terms: *Reflexivity, ethical hesitancy.*

As researchers, we frequently come to reflect on the kinds of stories we are producing or consuming, their contexts and what they mean, as well as their personal significance. Such self-reflection is often termed 'reflexivity'.

Reflexivity is apparent in the construction of stories, in general. Nakate's Dorcas story is self-conscious since the storyteller is aware of the story's effects on other people's lives. It is not just an independent 'story' in itself but a story artfully positioned in a certain political moment and in broader sociopolitical history. Forms of reflexivity can be apparent in many stories, particularly those where the storyteller refers to themselves.

Taking up the idea of reflexivity within research, narrative researchers often recognize themselves as active in the research process. Typical ways of being reflexive in research include:

1. considering why one might seek to research a particular topic, at times by writing on one's own relationship with it;
2. taking a position on the extent to which the interviewer ought to be actively shaping narrative texts and materials;
3. reflecting on the influence of the presence of the researcher in research, particularly in interviews and field observations, and considering how the research may impinge on the lives of the researched, during the research and in the dissemination of the research insights;
4. thinking about the relationship the researcher has with the research topic and participants, how our lived experiences frame our existing knowledge of it and how our different identity markers, such as gender, ethnicity, language or age, may affect these.

Reflexivity also allows the researcher to contemplate power relations and ethics in their research practices. Esin and Lounasmaa (2020; Lounasmaa et al., 2020) used the concept of ethical hesitancy (Kofoed and Staunæs, 2015), which means taking time to consider problems, power relations and ethical dilemmas as they appear instead of rushing to try and solve the issue. Engaging in collaborative art workshops with refugees in the Calais refugee camp, reflexivity regarding the gendered and racialized power dynamics within a context of extreme border violence became key. Recognizing our own shifting positionalities and relationships with participants created possibilities of trust and sharing. For instance, during the day, the white, Western female researchers could at times shield migrants from unwarranted police attention by their mere presence, whereas after sunset, we ourselves needed migrants to protect us in the camp. These dynamic power relations created opportunities for shared storytelling to arise as one of the 'technologies of resistance' (Foucault, 1998) available to the participants and the researchers together.

Reflexivity also has implications for how we conceptualize narrative research, specifically. For instance, taking on the idea that one has a story to tell of one's life experience implies a reflexive relation with narrative and, through it, with the self. In Vanessa Nakate's story, Nakate reflexively expounds on what she has learned from Dorcas's and similar stories and on how she can be those stories' conduit towards powerful effectiveness when she says 'my visit to Kenya allowed me to learn the stories of the people, and the children, behind the statistics. Stories like Dorcas's and Micah's', and then affirms, 'I will stand in for (children from the most affected areas) where they don't have a seat yet at the table, and tell their stories to those who have the power to bring real change'.

It is, therefore, possible to make yourself subject to narrative – the story told through you – and at the same time to make oneself the subject of narrative and to exercise its possibilities for establishing identity, relations with others and even, it seems, meaningful presence. Narrative researchers often focus on the instances and forms of such self-reflexivity in stories, reflecting on the kinds of subject positions that people seek to claim or reject, modify or resist. Narrative then draws attention to active subjects laying claim to identities and giving meaning to social experiences, but not outside the historical and social circumstances in which they find themselves. Not all narrative researchers are interested in or dwell on these matters, however. Researcher reflexivity will be more or less important, depending on the aims of the research.

How do these reflective practices, which are also ethical practices, relate to ideas about narratives' relation to social and political change? Many contemporary narrative researchers are concerned to do work that is sensitive to political and social conditions, that describes them clearly, fully, or in new ways, and that may also contribute to understanding or even promoting progressive social change (see, for example, Squire, 2021). This concern has led to considerable interest in the idea of counter-narratives.

E. What is a counter-narrative?

Key new terms: *Master narrative, counter-narrative.*

Master narratives structure how the world is intelligible and, therefore, permeate the smaller narratives of our everyday talk. Generally, speakers are compliant and only rarely engage in resisting or countering the grid of intelligibility provided by what is taken for granted (Bamberg, 2004: 361).

Henry Louis Gates has described counter-narratives as 'subaltern knowledge' and 'the means by which groups contest … dominant reality and the framework of assumptions that supports it' (Gates, 1995: 57). Abdi (2023: 70) suggests that in the context of narrative research, the history of counter-narratives within Critical Race Theory means that they are, generally, 'a response to majoritarian narratives and … lay the ground for activism'. Dominant or *master narratives* and *counter-narrative*s are not clear-cut, dichotomous categories but rather are thoroughly interwoven with one another. Stories always sit in relation to other stories. The accounts that people do and do not tell are often carved within the framework of what they take to be a shared master narrative, regardless of how they position themselves in relation to it.

While there has long been a recognition of the tension between stories, in the past two decades, scholars have become increasingly interested in theorizing this contestation. Bamberg and Wipff (2020) write that 'counter-narratives have come to occupy the center of many discussions regarding analytic work with narratives as related to power and social change' (p. 38). Hyvärinen returns to Bruner's (1990) much earlier work on the tellability of narratives which violate and discusses some of the shortcomings, which arise from universalizing canonical expectations. Using history writing as an exceptional case of master and counter-narratives, Hyvärinen suggests 'a move in empirical analysis from naming stories as master or counter narratives to analyzing the ways individual stories and storytellers *draw on* different master and counter narratives' (2021: 17).

Master or dominant narratives abound in all societies – functioning as the script by which members of the community are meant to fashion their lives. As Harris, Carney and Fine write,

> master narratives are often hard to see until you look under the covers – they are normally labeled as common sense and therefore become invisible in everyday life and academic productions ... master narratives do exist, and their real-life presence/impact is experienced with particular clarity by those for whom they do not speak and about whom they do not speak ... Master narratives set out guidelines for how stories should be told; how lives should be lived; how blame and merit should be allocated. (2001: 8–9)

Individuals and groups routinely articulate positions, which lie outside the boundaries of that which is expected, the normative. However, as Torre et al. (2001) write, 'critical stories are always (and at once) in tension with dominant stories, neither fully oppositional nor untouched' (p. 151). Similarly, Cavieres-Fernandez (2017), writing about Chilean teachers' narratives that counter the state's 'mega policy narrative' of citizenship education, identifies some counter-narratives that engage critically and oppositionally with the state narrative and others that focus on civic spaces distinct from but still 'alongside' state institutions.

Even when people do offer potentially resistant storylines, they tend to do so in a way which implicitly acknowledges the dominant framework and even strategically borrows from some of its components while rejecting others. An example of this can be seen in one of the more popular defenses of gay marriage, whereby long-term monogamous relationships are still upheld as the ideal, even while same-sex couples offer a variation on the traditional construction of marriage being between a man and a woman. While the meanings of counter-narrative or counter-stories remain contested (Elliot, Squire and O'Connell, 2017; Lueg and Lundholdt, 2021; Squire, 2024), scholars who use these terms do agree on the central importance of identifying master narratives and positions which fall outside what is assumed to be normative. These positions may themselves be 'inside' the master narrative, for such a narrative is often riven with internal contradictions that can be worked with critically – 'cracks' that will help transform societies (Cavieres-Fernandez, 2017).

Stories, then, are never only personal stories, but rather, they are situated in relation to the stories of others, both known and unknown. Critically, they are located within – even while they might challenge – the expected norms of a social group.

The potential for counter-narratives to open up new space is powerful:

> The power of master narratives derives from their internalization … [But] how can we make sense of our selves, and our lives, if the shape of our life story looks deviant compared to the regular lines of the dominant stories? The challenge then becomes one of finding meaning outside the emplotments which are ordinarily available. We become aware of new possibilities. (Andrews, 2004: 1)

Yet contestation is at the heart of counter-narratives, even while that which is dominant and that which is resistant are categories which are themselves forever in flux. A counter-narrative might not only be a different kind of story but even a different way of telling a story. It is not necessary that the master narrative which is being resisted is articulated, and the more dominant it is, the more likely it is that it will remain implicit. When narrative researchers embark on projects with others with whom they do not share common cultural referents, they may not be aware of the positional complexities of the stories they are hearing.

Examples of the importance and currency of counter-narratives saturate our news. Instances abound: the contrasting depiction of events, which occurred at the US Capitol on 6 January 2021 (were they patriots or insurrectionists?), the initial police report of the killing of George Floyd in contrast to the testimony of eyewitness which later emerged and the closing statement of Harvey Weinstein's defense attorney, in which she describes the prosecution's narrative as 'an alternative universe', are all examples of the contestation of narratives (and counter-narratives) in the public domain.

Although the term 'counter-narrative' is often used to demarcate a political positioning which challenges a conservative or regressive status quo, this is not always the case. Anders Brevik, the Norwegian mass murderer, offered a counter-narrative to normative multiculturalism in the justification he offered as an explanation for why he killed seventy-seven people. While he knew killing was wrong, he told the court that he did it 'in order to defend my country and my people'. In this reworking, the 2011 killings were both brave and selfless; one sees here the political power of attending to positioning, and repositioning, in narrative research vis-à-vis adopting other narrative frameworks (see Chapter 4, Section B, for other examples).

This chapter has introduced you to some general debates within narrative research. The next two chapters give you snapshots of narrative research in action in a range of fields. The debates we have considered play out across these applications. Not all of the debates affect every field, but you should be able to see them all at work at various points across the two chapters.

CHAPTER 3

Narratives in social research: Researching narratives across media

In this and the next chapter, we provide some examples of narrative methods being deployed in six different fields of social science research. We want to give you a 'road map' through some applications of narrative research to show you what this approach can, and cannot, deliver. Each example has been written by a researcher who has worked in the specific field for many years. In later chapters, we will call on these examples when we consider the uses of, challenges to and criticisms of narrative research. We cover the examples in two chapters, each with a particular contemporary significance within narrative research: narratives in different media and narratives' relations to power and resistance. As Chapters 1 and 2 have indicated, both these focuses are central to current narrative research debates.

This chapter, focusing on narratives across media, looks in more detail at what we consider to be narratives and where we look for them. These issues have implications for how we will choose to address narratives. Different research and analytic methods need to be brought into play when narratives are oral or written or enacted through the body, visual media or online, digital media. Moreover, our theoretical understanding of narrative may have to change if we are going to take narrative media seriously as themselves constituting narratives rather than simply reflecting or expressing them.

The following sections on recent narrative research in relation to the body, visual narratives and narratives and digital media demonstrate these shifts in the narrative research field. The sections progress from considering the body, which has always been an integral but often overlooked part of the personal narratives that form the basis of much narrative research; through to examining visual narratives, which have played a powerful part in people's lives and stories, especially since the development of print, photographic and broadcast media; to a focus on digital narratives, which are more and more central to people's personal and social lives as access to and influences of digital media expand.

A. Narratives and the body

This section addresses the much-researched field of narratives about the body. It interprets this field broadly to include narratives focused on bodily metaphors or analogies and narratives that use the body as part of their representational strategies – for instance, through tone of voice, gesture and silence. The section points up the importance of a specifically *narrative* analysis of the body in such representations, if we are to understand fully the meanings that the body carries within people's lives.

In much narrative research and theory, the bodies of both the storyteller and listeners, as well as of the characters appearing in the story, are taken for granted. Bodies are something that are always assumed to be there without having to be noticed, mentioned or commented on. Indeed, in these situations it may be difficult to identify and narrate what exactly the body is doing. It is only when the body becomes relevant to what is happening in the story that it merits descriptions and comments. For instance, in case of narratives about illness, violence or trauma, bodily transformations or physical disabilities, the body is a particularly salient aspect of verbal narratives. Alison Lapper's autobiography, *My Life in My Hands* (2006), beginning with her life as a severely physically disabled child in the 1960s, proceeding through to her work as an artist and a mother, is one instance. Nisreen Alwan (2021) describes how people's collective documentations of their own bodies' evidence of Covid-19 in the first years of the pandemic, particularly within online fora, generated recognition of and response to this condition, against considerable medical and political resistance. However, bodies have a more ubiquitous, though less-remarked, presence in narrative materials also.

In social research, stories are often collected either from interviews or from recordings of everyday situations. That is, stories are gathered in situations where the participants in the storytelling event are bodily co-present, making it possible for the participants to construct the meaning of the stories through the use of bodies as semiotic resources. Hence, in these situations it is valuable to focus the analysis not only on the narrative as text but also in the telling of the story; the ways tellers and listeners interact and, in particular, how they use their bodies as a resource in the telling (Goodwin, 2003; Kendon, 1990).

Both the storytellers and the listeners can use bodies in several ways: the body becomes an instrument for telling the story; for re-presenting events and actions (for further discussion about embodiment and storytelling, see L. C. Hydén, 2013, 2018a).

1. The *voice* is one of the most central bodily resources, although often taken for granted. The voice that presents the verbal story is rarely a neutral, mechanical voice, recapitulating a textual script. Rather, the voice is used to differentiate between different positions in the story: between various characters and their specific traits, as well as foregrounding the narrator guiding the listeners through the story. The voice can be full of warmth as well as sarcasm or other emotions, adding further meaning to the verbal text of the story, sometimes adding ironic comments or questions. Transcription can only go so far with conveying characteristics of voice. Changes in pitch are sometimes marked with up or down arrows and loudness with capitals. Pauses, an important aspect of voice, may be indicated by second measurements in brackets – for example, (2) to indicate a two-second silence. Non-verbal aspects of voice are frequently noted, too, bracketed in specific ways to indicate that they are not part of the verbal record, for instance, with [laughs] and [sighs]. However, researchers most interested in voice tend to work with the sound record rather than with transcripts.

2. The hands are used for *gestures*. Participants in storytelling events often sit or stand together in such a way that an interpersonal space is formed between them. This space can be used by all participants for gesturing. Some gestures are indexical, pointing out certain persons, tracing a movement in space. Other gestures use the interpersonal space in order to outline objects or aspects of objects and characters. Still other gestures are more conventional, such as displaying a peace sign or an 'OK' sign. Again, such gestures are hard to convey in written transcription. Researchers most attentive to them tend to use video data and may refer to time codes on their video records rather than trying to capture visuo-spatial elements verbally.
3. Also, other parts of the body are used, in particular, the eyes. Participants use their *gaze* to underline points, to signal interest and so on. The eyes together with the rest of the face are used for signalling surprise, joy or interest. The *positioning of the body*, for instance, moving closer to other participants, may indicate closeness and intimacy.
4. Both listeners and tellers are often caught up in *emotions* that emerge from the story, laughter and sorrow as well as feelings of wrongdoing or anger. Emotions are bodily stated, not only felt but also shown in various ways for the other participants to note, observe and share.
5. The body may be involved in more subtle ways as when *memories* are recalled. Although memories are often thought of as images, modern neurocognitive research shows that memories are better thought of as modal fragments spread in a vast neural network involving most parts of the brain. This means that all the body's senses – from motor memories to visual and smell memories – become involved both in telling stories about autobiographical memories as well as when listening to and sharing memories.

In addition to the telling of story, bodies are also re-presented in the storyworld as what we could call the *narrative body*. That is, most stories involve characters, and (most) characters have bodies. When the focus is on something other than the character's actual body, the body is taken for granted. As listeners, we tacitly assume that characters not only have bodies but that these bodies obey the same physiological and physical laws as all other bodies: persons cannot fly on their own and need to eat and sleep, and so on – although this is not stated explicitly in the story.

In many stories, especially in autobiographical stories, the content or theme of the story may be body related, as when a person falls ill, is hurt or a child grows and develops, or the body changes in other ways. It is when the body changes or is changed that the body or aspects of the body become noticeable, often as problematic or in some other way, both for the body's owner and for other persons at that point. The body is no longer something that can be taken for granted or presupposed. Bodily changes are something that demand comments and accounts. As a consequence, 'the body' is divided into the actual present body and the narratively re-presented body. This makes it possible for the owner of the body and others to comment on his or her own body as if it no longer belongs to or is a part of him or her.

When the body becomes thematized in the story, it must be explicitly represented, either by using the present physical body and pointing at it or by discursively describing the body using, for instance, metaphors or by using the body as a metaphor for describing and characterizing events.

Storytellers have an interesting possibility here, namely, using the storytelling event as a way to position the body of the actual storyteller in relation to one or several narrative versions of this body. The storyteller may even position his or her actual, physical and present body in relation to a different body that is severed from the actual body. This makes it possible to claim or dis-claim previous bodies and previous identities in the present and in relation to the present body and even to claim future bodies and identities in the present (something children often do when they talk about who and what they want to become or look like later on in life).

Telling stories not only involves a positioning of the actual physical body of the storyteller in relation to bodies in the storyworld, that is, the entirety of media and texts involved in the story. Storytelling also directly engages the bodies of both the teller and the listener. In the speech situation, the relation between the teller and listener changes as soon as the story begins. The teller and listener disengage from each other and their joint engagement is turned to the storyworld. In other words, although the participants are still aware of each other in the speech situation, their joint attention is tuned to the storyworld. They have become transported to the storyworld from the here and now of the speech situation. This transport not only is a journey of the mind but also includes the participants' bodies. The participants are transported to the storyworld through the performance of the narrative, and this transportation is embodied.

For the teller and listener, this means that they redefine their relation and the way they understand and interpret especially the teller's bodily movements. The teller's voice, gestures and other bodily movements have become subjugated to the events in the story and only serve to communicate what happens and to comment on these happenings. The listener's body closely follows the same events and registers all dramatic turns, tragic moments, suspense and sudden changes of luck. The listening to stories is an embodied process: tragic or comedic developments are not just registered cognitively but, above all, bodily by the listener as well as by the teller. Both participants are immersed in the story. This creates an emotional involvement in the storytelling and listening. When the events in the story induce suspense, the heart rate increases, tragedy results in tears and jokes result in laughs and rocking bodies. So, being 'transported' to the storyworld implies that the listener is bodily subjected to the events in this world.

B. Visual narratives

In the previous section, we have seen the many ways in which the body is a neglected but important, even ubiquitous, element of the practice of narrative research.

In a similar way, this section explores another resource, visual presentation and representation, that has a fundamental presence within everyday life. Visual narratives both present the self and tell about life. They surround us in many personal, local, national and international contexts and through global popular media. We progress daily through the narrative spectacles of markets and shopping malls, churches and other places of worship, museums and theme parks, factories, offices and graveyards. Photographs mark out our life stories from birth through marriage to, sometimes, death; they chronicle holidays, parties, celebrations and disasters. We watch film and television narratives regularly, and we may also make our own moving-image records of our lives and share these online. We scan newspaper and magazine stories, ads and fliers; we composite visual images into albums, scrapbooks and commonplace books. Even in written materials, the visual has a powerful place. Images from a written text may fall out of it like photographs or may sketch or compose themselves in our understanding like drawings or paintings. Interestingly, bodies are often central to the kinds of visual images (still and moving) that are used in, or are performative in, popular and everyday narratives. Equally, as noted above, the body itself presents visual cues and is also a site for visual work such as tattoos and visual readings of, for instance, dress and hair styles.

Alongside the growth in popularity of visual methodologies in social research, there has been rising interest in visual narrative research in the latter part of the twentieth century. Relatively early on, some researchers realized the potential of visual technologies as an aid to storytelling. The video diary was one such technology (see Rich and Chalfen, 1998) and was providing research participants with cameras in order to record and document their own lives or aspects of them – what is called photo-voice. Using such techniques provided a means for participants to control research data and more 'authentically' relate it to their own experiences, as opposed to being filtered through the research relationship of the interview. The use of disposable cameras has since been criticized, as it may indicate to participants that they are, just like the images they take and the cameras they use, disposable (e.g. Lounasmaa et al., 2020). In the current age of portable digital technology, most people already have access to digital cameras anyway. Visual narrative methods were often seen as an automatically emancipatory aspect of research. In fact, researchers usually remained in control, directing what they wanted (even if broadly defined) and also interviewing respondents about their images afterwards, thus reinscribing more traditional research power relations (see Chapter 4, Section A, where participatory research of this kind is discussed).

As with written texts, visual materials in narrative research can be found or elicited by the researcher. If elicited, they are part of a research relationship – often in combination with interviews. It is likely that both the production and use of elicited images will be around a particular topic in people's lives, and the visual materials are used to stimulate storytelling and meaning making. With photo-voice, photo-elicitation remains the most widely used visual methodology (Harper, 2002). Visual materials may also include asking people to share existing photographs or create images using any art-making techniques, such as maps, body maps, self-portraits (Esin, 2017), digital stories (Vacchelli, 2018), comic books. We know that many artists have often painted very personal aspects of their lives, the spaces which they inhabit, family members and selves. Researchers such as Tamboukou have found rich sources of narrative within the letters and paintings of Gwen John (Tamboukou, 2010), and the paintings of Frida Kahlo, and the illustrated nature of her diary, are narrative sources of her life with relationships, emotions and experience in visual evidence (Yang, 2002).

There is potential data, too, in photographic archives, which contain amateur personal images as well as those taken either officially or professionally. Langford (2001), using a Canadian museum collection of albums, some 'found' and of unknown origin, has argued that in their patterns of representation, inclusion and organization, they demonstrate the traditions of orality that have been drawn on by the compilers. These are albums with storytelling embedded in them. There are now collections of 'found' photographs, sourced, for instance, from junk shops on internet sites (see, e.g., www.foundphotography.com).

The practice of posting and reposting images, such as photographs and moving images, on a wide range of photographic and social networking sites such as Instagram and YouTube, has grown exponentially in recent years and these digital and social media platforms are now an important source of both textual and visual narratives. Smartphones have enabled the taking, editing, selecting and sharing to be possible for many to interact with others, things and places with such visual conversations becoming new forms of embodiment and social ritual. All these visual media may be seen as new cultural artefacts (See Burgon and Green, 2018 and Leaver, Highfield and Abidin, 2020).

There is now considerable attention paid to how we carry out research using digital methods and materials (Rogers, 2019; Rose, 2022; and Chapter 5), which narrative researchers need to consider. Moreover, digital image creators and commentators frequently act as 'researchers' themselves. Photograph and video-sharing sites often actively encourage the addition of comments, information and one's own story. Many Flickr, and now, Instagram, TikTok and Twitter or X users have formed groups around events such as disasters, providing personal storytelling that is now a form of public history (Harrison, 2010), with documentary and narrative evidence of experience. As image posting on social media is instantaneous, it competes with official news media and government-approved images of events, especially in places where censorship is high. These visual modalities can work as narrative co-constructions, with the exchanges of images and texts building narratives that extend beyond individual experience (see also Chapter 2, Section C).

It is in this way that digital media platforms, along with exhibitions and screenings, have become forums for many political and collective events of our time, such as Black Lives Matter, climate change and Covid-19, serving both social investigative purposes as well as individual and relational perspectives. In many respects, they exemplify how dialogic performances between narrators and audience are core aspects of visual narrative, and narrative generally. In them, 'small stories' of individual narrators become 'big stories', co-produced by many narrators (see Chapter 1, Section C).

Another kind of narrative, the counter-narrative (see also Chapter 2, Section E), can also be found utilizing visual media. Both Kuhn (1995) and Walkerdine (1991), for example, have used photographs of themselves as children from family albums as a way of coming to a new understanding of family relationships and lives and their own place within these. Their alternative readings or interpretations of these images reject the remembered collective narrative that had accompanied them. Traditions such as phototherapy also re-envisage family and personal relationships by creating new pictures which reject the conventionalized nature of family images as well as other kinds of counter-narrative. This kind of visual narrative work is not all progressive or intended to relate to reality. With the development of AI images, social media is increasingly contributing to making up alternative news – visual counter-narratives which are aiming to provoke, and often to mislead, their audiences. Visual counter-narratives thus operate oppositionally in many directions – not only because of their content but also because they challenge traditional uses of visual technologies of communication.

When thinking about using amateur images and visual practices in the research setting, some understanding of how images work in everyday contexts and lives is helpful, since the conventional nature of the production and consumption of images influences both what kinds of images may be found and their significance (Bourdieu, 1990). Images are particular symbolic traces of experience. They tell us some things and not others; they might be considered partial renderings of 'reality' (Harrison, 2002). There is a strong connection between photographs and memory in everyday life. For some people, photographs are the material representation of their memories; for others, they are cues for, or 'triggers' to, making sense of biographies over time. As such, they often require verbal/written narrations to make them meaningful and to allow those meanings to be available to others. For Barthes (1981: 82), the photograph does not call up the past; rather, it is a form of evidence 'attesting to what I see existed'. For others, photos do call up the past and then act performatively, constructing their meaning as they are viewed in the present. In news media, advertising and political messaging photos are used selectively to frame a certain type of story and characters.

An example of such clear selectivity we mentioned in Chapter 1 is the news agency photograph, which cropped out Vanessa Nakate. The image was taken by an Associated Press photographer at the end of a 2020 climate activists' news conference at Davos. Five young people, including Greta Thunberg, are standing outside, with mountains behind four of them and a building behind and to the side of Nakate. In the initially published photos from the event, the building and the only activist of colour in the picture, Nakate, were edited out on, the press agency said, 'composition' grounds. This account raises questions about racialized picture-editing conventions. It seems a background building may be visually problematic enough to warrant a cropping that also 'whites out' the African climate activist in the foreground.

There is an important question to be addressed about narrative and visual media. A number of writers have strongly suggested that the story or narrative lies behind or is buried beneath the image. In this argument, visual images are fragments that allow for the construction and reconstruction of auto/biographical and other narratives. This perspective is implied in the above discussion of photos as memory triggers. Berger and Mohr (1982: 107), for instance, suggest it is narrative which rescues the photographic image from its dislocation: 'a way of seeing which requires reassembling of the contexts of experience in which the photograph is embedded, the continuity from which it was taken'. This argument might raise doubts about whether or not images do narrate in their own right. Langford, whose work on photo albums we mentioned earlier, suggests that images may indeed have to narrate since, in many albums, at least, we have no one to fill in the absences.

Accessing this 'silent' story existing in the gaps between images, providing narratives of still images and providing verbal narratives of any visual image raises a problem of interpretive authority, which often seems much more acute across this media divide than it does when materials and analyses are verbal. The viewer or audience may read or narrate stories around images which are not necessarily those intended by their creators (although that is also the case with verbal stories). However, at times, images can express aspects of people's lives, relations and histories that are not verbally reachable and that have clear meanings. Shose Kessi's (2021) collaborative photo-narrative work with University of Cape Town students, exposing gendered and racialized pathways through a historically white university, for example, powerfully documented Black bodies' exclusions within that built environment in a way that descriptive writing would have been unable to do.

In practice, most narrative researchers use visual images, whether still or moving, to provide access to the wider story. The photographers in Kessi's study generated written texts to accompany the images. Wendy Luttrell's (2020) work with young people from migrant backgrounds in the United States, Susan Bell's (2009) study of generations of US women living with a reproductive health condition and Cigdem Esin and Corinne Squire's (2013) analyses of the visual autobiographies of people living in East London provide examples. Crow's (2022) study of UK academic retirees similarly combine data, in these cases from interview and ethnographic as well as visual narrative research.

There are stories about pictures and stories that lie between and behind them. At any particular time, individuals will have a particular relationship to an image or set of images. The meaning of those images can and will change. Memory, narration and the production of the self are all ongoing dynamic processes in the communication and social relationships of everyday life. As with oral or written texts, we may use visual images to access particular experiences or we may be interested in how the image itself works to produce meanings. Whether elicited or found, and using a variety of technologies of production, selection and analysis, image(s) are now established in narrative research, providing a rich source of material within the constraints of photographic and artistic practice. What we need to understand better, however, is how processes of transforming images into words occur. We also have to accept that not all images have value or even potential as (generators of) narratives. Criteria of validity and guidelines for analysing visual productions narratively still seem to be somewhat elusive. With increasing research in the area, we can expect many more contributions on these issues.

In summary:

1. Images are symbolic representations that can be analysed to reveal the meaning of everyday lives.
2. They may be past or present, found or elicited by the narrative researcher, with digital/social media providing new sources of visual narratives.
3. They can be a naturalistic resource for understanding a variety of topics, or they may be studied from a constructionist perspective, as topics in their own right.
4. Most often, narrative research will utilize images as just one component of the research design and will understand them as a means by which narratives can be constructed. Thus, there is usually assumed to be a symbiotic or dialogic relationship between image and written/verbal texts in this kind of research.
5. There are still questions to answer about how we should analyse visual productions and where their validity lies.
6. Attention will need to be given to ethical dimensions that are particular to visual methods, especially ownership, privacy and publication (see Papademas, 2009; Prosser et al., 2008).

C. Narrative and social media

We have seen in the previous sections how bodies can be implicated in storytelling and how the visual image can convey and/or inspire, even demand, narrative. Both cases suggest how embodied practices and visual media inhabit, sustain and give force to storyworlds. This section considers narrative research in relation to social media, helping to build our picture of different narrative modalities. Social media – Facebook, Instagram and TikTok, among other examples – due to their multimedia and interactive character, combine and extend how narratives are implicated in embodiment and the visual image. Social media also intensify the practices and meanings of copresence, since narrators and listeners need not be in the same physical space or time. Though they may see their interlocutors and hear their voices, narrators and their audiences are not necessarily seeing each other in real time, although some digital technologies such as Zoom and photo sites enable such copresent interaction. Social media also deepen narrative agency in specific ways since they incorporate the technological means of editing text, modifying images and videos and curating online presence and connections. While social media narratives may unfold in real time, they can have a longer life and possibilities of multiple readership and dissemination, rather different from those of the body narratives and many of the image narratives considered earlier in this chapter. Social media narratives also foreground interaction and social networks in specific ways, giving them, in some circumstances, a pronounced quality of co-narration and networked meaning. Nevertheless, as we shall see, some aspects of personal narratives are held in common across these divergent modalities.

In what follows, we discuss narrative and social media in relation to i) the narrative structures that social media make possible, ii) the meanings and effects thought to be attributed to social media narratives and iii) social media narratives as lenses on lived experience.

i) Structural analyses of social media narrativity

Analysts have considered how different kinds of social media shape narratives. Researchers using this approach are concerned with the affordances and productive disruptions that social media have for narrative practices. For example, De Fina (2016) has examined responses to blog posts to understand how storytelling is achieved and sustained interactively in social media. This analysis identified the framings of meaning established in the blog posts, how bloggers interacted with others' posts, the tone (aggressive, neutral, amicable, ironic) of the posts and if they combined texts with other media (pictures, videos). The analysis shows how bloggers cooperate (or not) with storytelling and the wider techno-cultural production of narratives.

In another example, Georgakopolou (2022) collected stories posted by an Instagram influencer and explored how the social media platform encourages and delimits kinds of storytelling practices. On Instagram, stories are shaped and circulated through the technical operation of the app in contact with the agency of the influencer and their responses to follower endorsements. Principles of 'sharing life in the moment' and 'authenticity' are also features of the Instagram influencer narration.

Analyses like these help us understand how narratives are (re)organized through different forms of social media technology and related aesthetic judgements, values and interactions, revealing both the continuous currents in narrative cultures and their new-found expressions.

ii) Meanings and effects of social media narratives

In the second mode of analysis, researchers focus on particular social phenomena linked with found social media materials and analyse their narrative properties. Like researchers focused on the social media narrative affordances *per se*, some researchers are concerned with what are thought to be the impacts of social media on social life. A useful example is #hashtag activism framed in terms of narrative agency. This research examines how digital storytelling builds in social media to address racism (#BlackLivesMatter), sexual abuse (#MeToo) and violence (#JeSuisCharlie), among other matters. Analysts typically collect tweets linked by these hashtags to consider the overall narrative form of the tweets over time, how these materials tell of a particular historical moment, how the hashtags and related tweets and tweeter connections express narrative agency, how the hashtags convene affective publics and how these effects inspire the sharing of stories to help collectivize and produce social force in public life. Giaxoglu's (2018) analysis of #JeSuisCharlie posts, including those responding to a single tweet by Salman Rushdie, showed how tweeters formed an affective community around the tweets. The #JeSuisCharlie hashtag operated as a powerful metanarrative of the violent incident that tweeters were able to re-inscribe, circulate and embellish in networked co-production. Similarly the Polish pro-choice movement used #BlackProtest (Nacher, 2021) to help mobilize resistance to neo-conservative restrictions on women's sexual and reproductive health rights and access to abortion. On this basis, Nacher (2021) reflected on the significance of digital feminism for action on social justice. Analysts have also shown how social media narratives can exclude identities and transform social movements. Trott (2021) examined the content of #MeToo tweets to show how narratives on sexual violence and Black African women had come to be displaced by a white-centred and celebrity narrative of sexual violence. Trott argued for caution with regard to the transformed meanings of #MeToo and its continued salience for feminism in general.

iii) Social media narratives and lived experience

Other researchers focus on lived experience in relation to social media. In this mode of analysis they might analyse found social media materials from a narrative point of view or elicit experiential narratives to understand life in post-digital worlds. For example, Jaworska (2018) examined Mumsnet.com blogs to understand how mothers disclosed and discoursed on postnatal depression. Jaworska, in particular, analysed confessional storytelling and moral injury and also how responses to these stories and sharing of personal experiences went some way towards helping bloggers repair their identities as mothers. This research demonstrated how social media narrative practices can reveal and transform lived experiences. In another example, Hammack et al. (2022) interviewed ethnic minority gay and bisexual men in the United States about their experiences of dating apps and the impact of stigmas related to race, gender performance, body shape and HIV serostatus. Following Bruner, the researchers conceptualized the interview materials as experiential narratives and developed an argument regarding 'intracommunity stigma' and how it is navigated by minority men in post-digital socio-sexual life.

Alongside these research approaches to narrative and social media is the canonical dual narrative of new technology-generated transcendence and decline, which relays into important questions of research conceptualization, consent, privacy, digital citizenship and ethical research practice. The rise of internet-based communications and digital and social media technologies has been met with a master narrative of either transcendence or fall, and sometimes both. Narratives on the transformative social, political and economic benefits of these communication technologies have been countered by narratives that, at least, signpost reservation, through to those that articulate fully fledged pessimism about society after social media. For example, it is implicit in research examining the impact of social media on narrative practices and in social worlds. But this dual canonical narrative can lead research into traffic with moral panic which may be unhelpful. It can also make it difficult to tease apart myth and justified criticism, a nuance that is imperative for examining the conditions of post-digital existence.

There are numerous moments in this dual canon of transcendence and declinism, but an important one is the 2018 Cambridge Analytica scandal (Bartholomeusz, 2018), in part due to its implications for research ethics and digital citizenship rights. The company and Facebook were exposed to have used user data without consent to model the social and psychological drivers of citizenship voting patterns. On that basis, the company promised expanded capacity to persuade voters in particular ways, a use of social media that attracted great monetary and political value. This particular event has drawn attention to the misuse of personal data, whether truly informed consent can be achieved, the ethics of using data without consent and related questions of digital citizenship rights to privacy and share in the monetization of personal information.

The Cambridge Analytica example is important because it points to practical, ethical and conceptual considerations for narrative researchers committed to sound and generative research inquiry. It also shows how social media narrative can itself be the object of productive analysis and a useful frame for research on social media narrativity, effects and lived experience.

The case studies in the chapter to follow develop these perspectives on narrative research practice and ethics. They do so by moving beyond everyday experience to consider narrative's connections with power and oppression, in particular, violence, gender, sexualities and activism.

CHAPTER 4

Narratives in social research: Researching narratives, power and resistance

We have seen many times already that narrative research is strongly implicated with ethical issues, partly because it often involves situations of personal or social injustice, partly because it may have antecedents or current interests in political movements such as feminism and partly also because its reflexivity and co-construction bring us to reconsider ethical and power issues throughout the research. We work with narratives as part of existing power relations and also as resistant, countervailing forces. We have to address narratives' mobility, their changeability across time and situation and their ability to shift between individual, social, cultural and political registers, always implicating the researcher along with the researched. These characteristics give narrative work a very particular relation to issues of power and resistance, which the following case studies from contemporary research demonstrate.

A. Narratives, violence and abuse

In this section we examine the place of narrative research in investigations of violence and abuse, specifically in the cases of gender-based violence and violence towards and abuse of children. We examine the significance of narrative research in understanding difficult aspects of these phenomena and in formulating successful responses. The section looks at children's ambiguous feelings in abusive families, women's relationships within situations of violence and family reactions to violence and abuse and points out how a narrative approach departs from and adds to other forms of research and practice in this field.

In his influential work *Telling Sexual Stories*, Ken Plummer (1995) argued that sexual stories, such as a story of rape, were for a long time not possible to tell, and if told, they were often not believed. The power of the political flow stopped any such attempts to tell or understand. Indeed, the #MeToo movement, which began in 2006 and gained worldwide recognition in 2017 after ousting Harvey Weinstein and numerous other men who held powerful positions in media and politics, showed us that stories of sexual abuse are still not tellable or listened to. Plummer's example shows that narratives are fundamentally co-constructed: without a real or imagined audience to listen, there are no narratives to be told. To narrate is a fundamental way of developing and communicating meaning. Patricia O'Connor (2000) has argued that there are three kinds of stories: *stories one likes to tell*, such as stories about graduating from college; *stories that must be told*, such as stories about practical issues; and *stories that cannot be told*, such as stories about sexual abuse. Stories about violence in intimate relationships belong to a fourth category, characterized by ambiguity, containing *stories that no one likes to tell, but that need to be shared* (Överlien and Hydén, 2003). These are stories about experiences of strange, painful and maybe confusing events. The need to narrate difficult and unfamiliar experience is part of the very human need to be understood by others, to be in communication even from the margins. Therefore, attention to human suffering means attention to stories.

Experiences of domestic abuse and violence were, for a long time, a particularly hidden element of human suffering. The contemporary conception of intimate partner violence is, to a great extent, a product of the feminist movement of the 1970s. When women stepped forward and began to talk about their experiences of violence, they thought they were talking from the margins. They had kept their experiences secret, as *stories that cannot be told*. Once abused women started to talk and found out that they shared their experiences with others, the stories were re-categorized as *stories that no one likes to tell, but need to be shared*, for political as well as personal reasons. However, this did not happen until the political flow made it possible for women to step forward and communicate painful experiences of a place that is supposed to be safe: the home. When women congregated in women's political and consciousness-raising groups and shared their personal experiences, it was revealed that they shared the experiences of being victimized by violence. They had previously kept this hidden, since they had seen it as an individual problem, as a personal failure. Suddenly, they had an audience listening to their stories; suddenly, experiences of violence became experiences they had in common with other women (Pizzey, 1974).

Talk about traumatic experiences, such as being a victim of violence or sexual abuse, has the potential to heal if the victimized is offered a safe space and given the opportunity to share his or her experience with someone who is prepared to listen. However, the attitude of the listener and preparedness to listen are crucial. While telling the story may be beneficial for the teller, narrative research interviews should never be treated as counseling, even in cases where the interviewer has counseling qualifications. The purpose and the setting of the interview, the fact that it is usually a one-off and the different role the interviewer plays here means that whatever benefits may arise can never be taken for granted or offered as a justification for such interviews. Talk about traumatic experiences also has the potential to pose a threat and even to re-traumatize the traumatized, just as much as it has the potential to heal.

i. Performing 'the battered woman'

When a woman is beaten by her husband, she not only suffers through his use of violence but is also inscribed in certain categories of persons, such as 'victim' and 'battered woman'. Even if she meets a researcher ready to listen, who works hard to create a space where she can safely tell her story, she might be reluctant to share her experiences of violence and perform 'the battered woman':

> To think of yourself as a battered woman ... that is almost impossible. I feel so ashamed ... to me a battered woman is an

unloved woman. I think this is why a woman doesn't want to go to the grocery store with a black eye. She doesn't want people to think: 'See, there is a woman whose husband beats her. See, there is an unloved woman' ... It's simply a way to protect yourself. (M. Hydén, 1995: 131)

In this interview excerpt, the interviewed woman vividly expressed her apprehension about seeing herself as a woman of low value. In her view, it was not the violence that placed her in a low position but the message it carried: *You are unloved*.

The women in this study by Margareta Hydén expressed the significance of being involved in activities of culturally low value, even if you were forced into them; even if you were a victim of them. Another woman in the study refused to perform 'the beaten woman with a miserable childhood'. She didn't like to talk about the fact that she had been beaten by her husband, even more so, because of her problematic childhood story. 'People don't want to look forward', she stated, 'if they find out about problems and misery, they really think they know something about you, just get down in all that trash and stay there, that's what they want you to do' (M. Hydén, 1995: 131).

When researching family violence and abuse and asking people to tell their story, we must be prepared to listen to a story of severe human suffering. To be assaulted is to be subjected to an illegal action and confronted with one's own helplessness and powerlessness. But it also requires confronting one's own actions, aimed at protection and resistance.

Some experiences of trauma and violence can also be unnarratable because we are not able to make sense of these events as they are unfolding. As we discussed in Chapter 1, the act of narration is an act of sense-making, where we choose relevant events, place them in a sequence and structure our story in a way that makes sense to us and fits our image of ourselves and the surrounding world. In her short film *A Letter to a Turtledove* (2020), Dana Kavelina superimposes archival footage of mining activities in Donbas under Soviet rule in the 1930s, found footage of the Russian invasion of the city in 2014, her own stop-motion animations and a letter, written to Donbas as if she was a woman whose body these different invasions and excavations were targeting. There is no linearity or clear sequence to the events; they happen simultaneously, over and over again, and they are not resolved through the telling. War violence has no meaning, and in the time of the making of the film there is no resolution or end, and hence these events and experiences evade narration.

A narrative researcher who is not prepared to listen to the story in its full complexity may miss the whole story because the person who has experienced violence does not want to perform 'the victim'; or they may get a very reduced story. Given the fact that life-story narrative in itself forms identity, there is a risk of being 'concealed into one's suffering' (hooks, 1999). Through the construction of 'victim' as a homogeneous and monolithic concept, the 'battered woman' is at risk of reducing her sense of self to one single characteristic: that of being battered.

'There are no relations of power without resistance', states Michel Foucault (1980: 142). In narrative research on interpersonal violence, this statement could be developed and transferred into the design of an interview that opens up the space for examining the relationships between male violence and female resistance by focusing on *agency* in a very specific sense, that is, the relationship between power, responsibility and activity as reflected in the various ways the interviewed women who had been battered *responded* to the violence.

ii. Opening the space for a complex story of 'the battered woman'

Responses could be of various kinds. One of the most powerful and visible for others is when women break up with and leave their abusive men. Responses that are rooted in fear, that compel silence, may be visible only as withdrawal and a minimum of cooperation and communication but may become more and more rooted in hatred and vindictiveness. One famous example is published in J. C. Scott's (1990) work on the responses to violence that cannot be expressed openly but nevertheless exist as 'hidden transcripts'. The example is drawn from slavery in the antebellum US South. Mary Livermore, a white governess from New England, recounted the reaction of Aggy, a normally taciturn and deferential Black cook, to the beating the master had given her daughter. The daughter had been accused, apparently unjustly, of some minor theft and had been beaten while Aggy looked on, powerless to intervene. After the master had left the kitchen, Aggy turned to Mary, whom she considered her friend and said:

> Thar's a day a-comin'! Thar's a day-comin!
> I hear the rumblin ob de chariots! I see de flashin ob de guns! White folks' blood is runnin on the ground like a ribber, an de dead's heaped up dat high!
> Oh Lor! Hasten de day when de blows, an de bruises, and de aches an de pains, shall come to de white folks, an the buzzards shall eat dem as dey's dead in de streets.
> Oh Lor! Roll on the chariots, an gib the black people rest and peace.
> Oh Lor! Gib me de pleasure ob livin till dat day, when I shall see white folks shot down like de wolves when dey come hungry out o' de woods. (Scott, 1990: 5)

The precondition for this part of the 'hidden transcript' to be openly delivered was the trust Aggy felt for Mary and that once the master had left, the kitchen was a safe space for the women to say what was in their hearts.

In line with Mary's and Aggy's relationship, the researcher and the researched need to be recognized in relation to each other. Without being able to construct a framework and a relationship in which the abused can feel free and have the opportunity to discuss her or his thoughts and feelings, the research ambition to listen to a more complex story is doomed to fail. In order to achieve that, a 'teller-oriented' (M. Hydén, 2014) model for interviewing is the most suitable. This model is based on the assumption that the research interview is a relational practice that places at the informant's disposal a framework for extending her understanding. The researcher aims at gaining access to her associations, her inner logic and understanding, or possibly her absence of inner logic and understanding, about what happened (M. Hydén, 2014). A research interview constructed in this way has many similarities with a therapy session, with one decisive exception: there is no agreement in the research interview to strive to achieve change. Having said that, the potential for change must not be underestimated in a research situation constructed so that, for instance, as in this case, a woman is requested to describe her experience to another woman who is present in every sense of the word. The researcher has also declared, in advance, that the narratives are so valuable that they will form a basis for expanding gendered knowledge about men's violence against women and about racist violence, as in Aggy's story.

iii. Stories of social networks' responses

Involved in women's stories about their responses are stories about how their social networks responded. The responses could constitute obstacles or be valuable resources (Hydén et al., 2020). The following excerpt illustrates this. The narrator is a thirty-year-old woman who is married to a man who subjected her to violence in connection with alcohol and drug abuse. She compares the responses in the countryside in a working-class environment with the responses in the city in an upper-class environment the family has moved to. When they lived in the countryside, the responses were very helpful:

> Well, in the country, the working-class mums were so used to their hard drinking men, so they had ways of dealing with intoxicated violent men and helping each other. When we lived there and they saw him drunk, they responded, 'Well, he's drunk. We will take care of her so she doesn't get hurt'. They never looked down on us because of that.
>
> Our daughter went to the nursery. It wasn't too great, but they were very good at dealing with parents with alcohol and drug problems. They were very observant, and if they saw Andrew under the influence, they called me and told me that he could not be entrusted with picking her up. Then they called the police. And sometimes the police responded by arranging a checkpoint at the little dust road he was driving. And he got caught, of course. It happened more than once. He never found out about what happened! He kept saying, 'I cannot understand this, checkpoints in the middle of nowhere. I must be the most check-pointed rural guy in the country' (laughter). (M. Hydén, 2015: 1051)

In the city, things were different:

> Here, in the city, it is different. He is sober at the moment, but I have thought 'if he starts, shall I tell my daughter's pre-school

teachers or the parents of her friends?' In the rural place we lived before, that had been most helpful, but here in the city I don't think anything good will come out of that.
That's the difference between the social classes. People in the working class drink a hell of a lot too much but learn to handle it. People in the upper classes drink too much too, but they are very shameful about having have alcohol problems, so they never learn to deal with it. Well, I know, it is my own homemade theory, but it has been proved to be right many times. (M. Hydén, 2015: 1051)

The consequence of this woman not daring to entrust herself to people in her new social context was that she became more vulnerable when she made the decision to leave the man.

iv. Children's stories of witnessing violence

Acts of violence against women take place not only in adults' lives but also in children's lives. Violence is something children experience from a position as subjects – not as objects, as concepts such as 'witnessing' or 'being exposed to' may suggest. The violent episode is situated in a larger context, the child's living environment, and is not something to which the child can merely be a passive witness. In a study based on children's narratives and focusing on their action when experiencing violence (M. Hydén, 2010; Överlien and Hydén, 2009), children said that they responded to the violence in different ways. The older children often tried to intervene, in order to try to stop the violence. The younger children tried to hide and escape the violence by blocking it out. They ran into another room, hid together in one of the siblings' beds and/or used music and books as a way of blocking out the sounds of violence and distracting themselves. These strategies were only partly successful: they escaped from seeing the violence but were usually forced to listen. A little boy, four at the time of the incident and ten when he tells the other children in a group interview said:

Once I put myself and the dog in the big room, once when mum and dad were fighting ... I turned on the TV and I watched the TV and shivered like crazy ... I mostly heard dad screaming.

I heard it in spite of the TV. If I had only known how to use the remote control I would have turned the volume up. (M. Hydén, 2010: 140)

In this short story, the young boy positions himself as someone who actively responds to the violence, not as someone who passively witnesses it. He gives his audience no orientation concerning the circumstances for his action but goes straight on to a brief presentation of the action to which his actions responded ('mum and dad were fighting'). He tells about his actions ('I put myself and the dog in the big room'; 'I turned on the TV') and how they failed ('I mostly heard dad screaming'). At the end of his short story, he gives a suggestion for a resolution ('If I had only known how to use the remote control I would have turned the volume up'). This way of positioning oneself – as an actively responding being – was characteristic of the children's stories. While parents had a tendency to position their children as passively witnessing the violence or sleeping (M. Hydén, 2010), the children talked about their actions in response to the violence. It is important for a narrative researcher to take into consideration that the existence of only one account of such an event is rare. After a round of interviews about an event, in all probability, the researcher will be equipped with a series of narratives out of which some will be in accordance with others, and some will be contradictory.

B. Narratives, sexualities and power

This section examines how narratives can help us understand sexuality as a social and cultural construct, interrelated with power relations and practices of dominance, submission and resistance. Like the previous section, which related narrative work on violence to analyses of specific gendered, generational and classed power relations, this section positions narrative work on sexualities in relation to earlier discourse-based research on sexualities and to feminist and queer-theory sexualities research. Here we analyse 'sexuality' as a category of knowledge that frames what we know about sexualities more generally; we relate narrative work to the work of Foucault on discourse and sexuality; and we look at the social power relations that shape sexual narratives.

As noted in *Telling sexual stories*, Plummer (1995) analyses the social conditions that have facilitated the emergence of new sexual stories. Plummer examines how telling sexual stories, as well as other stories, is closely linked to the social worlds in which experiences and narratives are constructed. Applying a similar approach, this section explores how narrative analysis can help researchers understand the interconnections between individual stories of 'sexuality', an intimate and personalized realm, and the broader sociocultural and political contexts of sexualities.

Here, we focus on Foucault's (1998) account of bio-power and adopt a Foucauldian discourse approach (Tamboukou, 2013) to narratives, drawing on examples from Cigdem Esin's (Esin et al., 2013) research on sexual narratives of educated young women and their mothers in Turkey. This approach allows a detailed microanalysis of individual stories of sexuality, positioning these stories within historical, sociocultural and political contexts.

The discussion in this section revolves around two main components of the analysis: first, the interaction between micro-sexual stories of participants and macro-narratives, attentive to larger contexts of gender, femininity and sexuality; second, the positioning of the storyteller and audiences that shapes every story at various levels, a more intimate level of context.

i. Analysing the interaction between micro- and macro-narratives

In this approach, situating the narratives within a historically specific context is the first step of analysis. The discourses of women's identities, sexuality and gender that were introduced within 'Turkish modernization' formed this context. Turkish modernization was a political and sociocultural project during the nation-state formation processes of the early twentieth century. Women were mobilized in the public sphere as professionals, educators and symbols of cultural transformations, and as asexual citizens, during these processes. Sexual modesty became the condition of possibility for women's public presence. Women's sexuality was, therefore, a site of disciplining regulations, which shaped modern women's identities within the broader sociopolitical project.

The analysis explores how the grand narratives of gender, women's sexuality and regulations were deployed and contested in participants' narratives. In the example below, Guzin constructs her story within a network of modernist narratives linking sexuality, the conditions of public presence for a woman and disciplinary practices in education and family reputation.

Guzin: ... Well, my father was a civil servant. He was a modern, open-minded man. Yet, he wouldn't let me go to university after high-school. He thought that I was educated enough, and that it was time for marriage.
... My parents were worried that I might have a relationship. I was beautiful, lively (smiling).
... There were already families who asked for my hand when I was at high school. I was very careful at school. I mean I had male friends, and admirers (err) but I was very careful. I didn't go out for lunch or have coffee with any male friends alone. I was allowed to go to the cinema or theatre as a group ... I'm glad that I was so careful. It was about my reputation after all. When my current in-laws decided to ask for my hand, they made enquiries at the high school where I was a student. They were told that I was well-taught, modest and did not flirt with anyone. My husband told me later (smiling) that's when they made up their mind.

At the time of the interview, Guzin was a housewife in her late forties who had not had higher education because of her father's decision. Secular institutions of education played a crucial role in the realization of sociocultural transformations within Turkish modernity. However, education was accessible for young women only as a package, which included the disciplining of femininity and sexuality, the main components of the modern patriarchal system. Women's experiences of education in mixed-gender institutions, in particular, were framed by the continuous concern of families about their daughters' contact with men. In Guzin's youth, mixed-gender higher education was available to the daughters of 'progressive' families. However, the concern of even some 'open-minded' families like Guzin's about their daughters' sexual reputation was so strong that higher education was not an option. In the rest of the excerpt, Guzin herself takes up a position within the dominant narrative of 'modern and/but modest women' while telling her story about her marriage. She talks about the marriage as a family arrangement, emphasizing that it was her well-disciplined femininity at high school that opened her path to marriage, usually perceived as a better status for a woman in her generation than being a spinster with a career. And she describes disciplining herself as a schoolgirl by keeping her contact with boys to a minimum, following the regulations that constantly reminded young women of the importance of her and her family's social reputation.

This analysis draws on the sociocultural and political macro-narratives defining women's sexuality in Guzin's youth, and subsequently, in which personal narratives such as Guzin's are constructed. Narrative analysis enables the researcher to focus on the way the storyteller configures her/his individual narrative in an interaction with the available macro-narratives and other cultural resources. This interaction is also shaped by the power relations of the research: the storyteller negotiates how her/his story can function in a dialogue with audiences, including the researcher. For instance, she is able to tell the researcher, a Turkish woman a generation younger than she was: 'I'm glad that I was so careful. It was about my reputation after all', without needing to explain further. Yet, at the same time, she can talk smilingly to the researchers about how 'beautiful, lively' she was and can be confident that this, too, is understood as she means it. Taking up Chapter 2, Section C's suggestions for translation in narrative research as 'intimate listening' exercises, in this case, the story is told in the storyteller's mother tongue, the same language in which the original interactions took place and within a cultural context that is shared between the teller and the listener, thus removing the need for cultural or linguistic translation at the point of interaction, or even at the point of analysis.

As was discussed in the previous section in relation to the research on responses to abuse, the commitment of the researcher to listen to the story carefully, familiarize themselves with the context and be willing to hear all the nuances are key to analysing the interaction between micro- and macro-narratives which makes a story function. For instance, Guzin's story, which is situated within the network of dominant storylines on disciplining sexuality, does not necessarily tell us that she would have preferred a marriage to having higher education if it had been her own decision. Despite her success story about how she negotiated her own marriageability, she does not explicitly take up her father's position on marriage. A further reading of her opening lines about her father's decision on her education, in connection with other parts of her interview where she talks about how women have to make their own decisions on their career and marriage, tells us that the way she integrates the macro-narratives into her individual narrative is not static. An individual narrative may simultaneously reiterate and counter the macro-narratives. As we have discussed in previous sections on counter-narratives, master/dominant narratives and counter-narratives are relational. Counter-narratives and counter-positions can sometimes be found blended into master narratives, particularly when we analyse intimate and personal narratives such as stories of sexuality and abuse.

What the narrative researcher needs to do is to make a close scrutiny of the power relations that continuously construct and reconstruct both micro- and macro-narratives. As we have discussed in previous sections on reflexivity in Chapter 2 and via other research examples in this chapter, power relations on various levels are part of narrative analysis. Another way to examine how power relations shape the narrative is to analyse positioning of storytellers and audiences in relation to each other and broader context.

ii. Analysing positioning in the construction of sexual stories

The analysis of positioning is often used in discourse as well as narrative analysis in order to understand how individuals draw on specific discursive resources and relations while talking about their lives. It is part of the narrative approach, which argues that individuals locate themselves in specific 'subject positions' while telling stories. These subject positions are informed by the social, cultural, linguistic, political and interpersonal resources available to individuals (Davies and Harre, 1990; Phoenix, 2013). Positioning analysis, as a methodological tool, helps the narrative researcher explore how the subject positions chosen by individuals are constituents of narratives.

The sexual stories research traced the movement of storytellers between multiple positions. The analysis focused on how research participants moved between choosing and chosen subject positions in relation to sexual regulations. This focus is useful in order to understand sexual stories as young women's negotiations within strong patriarchal hierarchies rather than as expressions of their docility within these hierarchies. The example below shows another participant, Bulut, reflecting on her repositioning within the modern gender regime.

> Bulut: My sister is three years older than me. She has always had boyfriends. She was hanging around with them. I was like the good girl, setting her in order. My dad was so strict about it ... We had unspoken rules at home. We all knew that we could not have boyfriends ...
>
> There were popular girls and boys at school. They were going out with each other. I wasn't one of them. I was a moderate girl with long socks, long skirt, wearing a boy's shirt with short hair. There was no atmosphere to be otherwise. I was going home after school. My mum was working then. I was taking care of my younger brother, doing my homework in the evening and going back to school in the morning. There was nowhere I could meet boys ...
>
> Later, I started to go to classical music concerts at the weekends. It was like a blossoming for me. I asked for permission to go. My dad didn't like it. He questioned me. With whom was I going there? I was going with a close girl friend ... It was my second year at high school, and my first real encounter with men ...
> 　I felt relieved outside home by these outings. I hadn't had any problems with my family until then. The problems started with these concerts. To that point, I was (errr), compared to my sister, more modest, more respectful to parents, more serious whereas she was loose, lazy, and unsuccessful.

Bulut was a vivid storyteller with a highly analytical voice, which was shaped by the feminist perspective that she and the researcher shared. The story above is from a longer narrative of her repositioning of herself within the gender regime of contemporary Turkey. Bulut tells of tensions she experiences in leaving her 'good girl' position in search of a space of freedom outside the home. In so doing, she portrays her sister and herself as representatives of two storylines of femininity. The basic criterion for being a 'good' or a 'bad' girl is defined by the degree of contact with boys. The restrictions on Bulut's everyday routine are an important set of disciplinary practices, constructing her as a 'good girl'. These practices are organized around regulations of time and space. Her weekdays are strictly scheduled between home and school, the sites of two institutions where she would be disciplined as a young woman. Unlike her sister, she does not have time to 'hang around' with her friends. Her insistence on going to concerts despite the risk of jeopardizing her relationship with her family is how Bulut tells us she negotiates between the strict reality of regulations and her dream of freedom. This position is not straightforwardly dominant or marginal. In telling us her story of resistance, she makes it clear to the audience that she acted appropriately by asking her father's permission and going to the concerts with a girlfriend, not a man.

Analysing positioning enables narrative researchers to understand how particular stories function within particular networks of power relations. As the example above demonstrates, there may be clear-cut positions available within power regimes, such as those of 'good' and 'bad' girls. Yet an analysis of positioning in micro-narratives such as Bulut's enables the researcher to understand how narratives open up a discursive space where storytellers negotiate their positioning, within but also beyond the power relations that constantly work on them.

C. Narratives and politics

The first quarter century of the twenty-first century has been marked by an increasing interest in what can broadly be termed 'political narratives' (Andrews, 2017a; Bradbury, 2019; Polletta, 2006; Plummer, 2019; Selbin, 2010; Squire, 2021; Zingaro, 2009). This phenomenon can be seen as one manifestation of the ballooning study of narrative generally within the academy, though – as we explored in Chapter 1, Section 2 – narrative social research seems significantly to have shifted its focus towards social justice and transformation within this time. While there is no strict consensus over what is and is not to be regarded as a political narrative, there appears to be agreement that stories – both personal and communal – are pivotal to the way in which politics operates, both in people's minds (i.e. how they understand politics and their place within and outside of the formal political sphere) and in how politics is practiced. These stories are not just within the domain of the individual but are built upon the collective memory of a group. They help to create how that memory is mobilized and for what purposes. This chapter subsection will explore examples of how this narrative approach adds to existing social-research approaches to political phenomena.

Before examining examples of political narratives, let us first explore more generally what is meant here by the term political narrative. For our purposes here, we will direct our attention to (1) the micro level: stories which are articulated by individuals about politics; (2) the macro level: the national political stories, enshrined in holidays, monuments and history textbooks; (3) the interactions between these two levels.

Stories which can be told, be they political or otherwise, are always predominantly the terrain of individuals, but all persons are ultimately part of wider social networks. Thus, while it is individuals who remember or forget, it is communities which heavily influence what is deemed memorable or forgettable. Examples of these memories and forgettings abound – as people recall their experiences of being in Berlin the night the Berlin Wall was opened, their memories of learning of the assassination of John F. Kennedy or their encounters with the global Occupy movement. But equally, people engage in political storytelling on numerous occasions, which do not appear to have anything to do with politics, at least not overtly so. If by politics one means the negotiation of power, then a significant number of stories could be classified, broadly, as political narratives.

Macro political narratives, in contrast, refer to the 'cultural stock of plots' (Polletta, 2006), in other words the contexts which make some stories more tellable than others. Although sometimes these are explicitly articulated, in history textbooks or in addresses made by public officials marking certain events, they derive much of their impact from the fact that often they are simply taken for granted. So, passing through Trafalgar Square in the centre of London, one does not need to know the details of the Battle of Trafalgar to be able to recognize that it must be an important piece of the story Britain tells itself about who it has been, and the outstanding contributions of certain of its citizens. But public spaces and the stories they tell are always contested. In June 2020, when persons who were participating in a Black Lives Matter protest in Bristol toppled a statue of seventeenth century slave trader Edward Colston and rolled it into the sea, they were demanding a different political narrative about Bristol be on display – and had indeed been demanding this, in Bristol, for over a decade.

Finally, the term 'political narratives' often refers to the dynamic movement between individuals and wider social contexts, or, in the words of C. Wright Mills, between biography and history. When Marx asserted that people make history, but not in circumstances of their own choosing, he was remarking upon this fundamental relationship between the micro and macro units of analysis, which ultimately lead to one another. But it is not always possible to discern the demarcation between the two. While each of us may be special or unique in some ways, still we recognize that everything we do is located within a wider social web of relationships and all of these within the complex matrices of social structures. Equally, there is nothing of politics that exists independent of identifiable human beings. One does not need to embrace the cult of the individual to recognize that even those persons who are known to us only through the media have private thoughts, desires and relationships. For instance, one would not be able to understand the actions of militant suffragette Emily Davison as she threw herself under the King's horse at the Epsom Derby in 1913 without contextualization; her suicide would be meaningless in the absence of the broader movement. And while a social movement is always bigger than the sum of its individual members, it is nonetheless comprised of real people with real lives. Sometimes, their individual stories, and sacrifices, become transformed into a symbol of the movement.

Let's now turn to some examples, so we can explore these issues in a more concrete way.

i. Example 1

The first example comes from an interview with Rosa Parks, who became famous around the world as the woman who, in 1955, refused to go to the back of the bus because of the colour of her skin. This small, defiant act kicked off the Montgomery Bus Boycott, a critical moment in the explosion of the civil rights movement in the United States. Popular folklore has it that Parks was almost an unknowing actor, tired and weary on entry to the bus and spontaneous in her refusal. That she was the secretary of the Montgomery chapter of the NAACP is not so well known, nor that she had been selected to perform this challenge. But listening to her account of this event puts the 1955 encounter with the bus driver, James Blaike, in another perspective. She recalls:

> About 12 years before this, about 1942, this same driver had evicted me from his bus for refusing to hand him my fare and then get off of the bus and go around and try to find my way back in the bus by the rear door. Because I refused to do that, he evicted me from the bus. He didn't call the policemen that time. He just told me I couldn't ride his bus. I told him I was already on the bus, and I didn't see any need of getting off and going around to the back door to try to get in, but that was one of the things he demanded. It was the very same driver, because I never did forget his face from that time on. I don't think he remembered me at the time I was arrested. (Parks in Wigginton, 1992: 233)

This small passage raises a number of questions for the reader, and a scrutiny of it begins to demonstrate the power of political narratives. Briefly, let's focus on three key elements: (1) time and timing; (2) agency; and (3) the intersection of biography and history.

1. The question of time is critical here. Parks alerts her listener to the fact that not only was the refusal in 1955 not her first, but it was not even her first with this bus driver. Indeed, they had already performed their respective roles, though not in an identical fashion, more than a decade earlier. Parks was not, then, an unknowing actor. This leads us to the second point.
2. In Parks's account, she is a very active agent in her own destiny. In 1942, she speaks back to the driver, who demands her eviction. Although she departs from the bus, she is not 'finished' with him, as history will tell us.
3. This story, interesting though it is, derives at least some of its impact from the knowledge that we as readers have, that

Parks could not have had in either 1942 or even 1955, that this action lit a powder keg of political resistance. In 2005, she died a national hero, the first woman ever to be granted the posthumous honour of lying in state in the US Capitol Rotunda.

ii. Example 2

The second example comes from an interview with Rose Kerrigan, one of the founding members of the Communist Party of Great Britain in the early part of the twentieth century. Kerrigan was interviewed by Molly Andrews in the mid-1980s (Andrews 1991/2008), who asked her about her earliest engagement in political activity. Kerrigan began by describing the poverty in which she and others lived in Glasgow in the early 1900s.

> I remember as early as seven or eight years of age, and thinking that it was very odd that here were so many people who could afford to be dressed up. We lived around the corner from the Royal Theatre ... we used to go down and watch them go into the theatre from the taxis and wonder ... here we could hardly buy our own shoes. That made me feel that there was something wrong, somewhere. Why did these people not share their money with us? ... I never felt anger and I never felt envy. I just felt it was wrong somehow ... at 12 years old I took part in the 1915 rents strike in Glasgow. [when Rose tried to convince her mother to withhold the extra rent] she said 'we'll run into debt and we'll never be able to get out of it. I said to her 'you give the extra money to me and I'll bank it.' Then when I saw I couldn't convince her by myself I went up the whole close which was 16 tenants and got them all agreed to withhold the rent and we never ever paid that increase. When the rent-man came for the rent, we paid the rent but we never paid the increase ... The result was the 1915 Rent Restriction Act which lasted till 1957. There weren't increased rents.

This excerpt, with its rich detail, provides much for one who is interested in political narratives. Here, we will focus on: (1) Kerrigan's perception of her young self; (2) the importance of relative deprivation and responses to the perception of social inequality;

(3) challenging ideas of childhood and political efficacy; and (4) the nuts and bolts of the birth of an effective social movement.

1. Freeman argues that 'narratives, as sense-making tools, inevitably do things – for people, for social institutions, for culture, and more' (2002: 9). A critical question is what this story actually accomplishes. Why does Rose Kerrigan tell it? This story positions the young Rose as someone who not only perceived injustice but also acted to fight against it. Even at the age of twelve, she was someone who put her principles into action (something which would continue to be a cornerstone of her identity for the next seven decades). Neither was she someone who would shy away from authority, be they the landlord, her mother or others in years to come.

2. Rose situates the story of her youth in a very particular setting. Living around the corner from Glasgow's Theatre Royal, she and her siblings would watch people as they arrived at the theatre in taxis. The affluence of others was especially marked in comparison to the economic hardship that her family and her neighbours knew. 'Why did these people not share their money with us?' she asks. One can hear in these words the seeds of a socialist consciousness. Rose portrays herself as someone who is not envious or angry but simply fair-minded. She emphasizes time and again that the disparity in wealth was simply wrong.

3. The construction of the child activist makes a particularly strong impression. Effective activism is always impressive, but it is especially so if that person is not even yet in their teenage years. That she would organize the rest of the close into collective resistance speaks volumes for the importance of small actions.

4. This story, like that of Parks above, derives some of its impact from the retrospective knowledge of the role of the Glasgow Rent Strike of 1915, in which 30,000 people eventually withheld their rent from profiteering landlords.

In the examples of Rosa Parks and Rose Kerrigan, the individual account helps to shed light on wider social and political processes. In both instances, the women position themselves as knowing political actors in a contest which ultimately they would win. The accounts themselves add texture and invite further reflection on key political events, the Montgomery Bus Boycott and the Glasgow Rent Strike.

Political narratives matter immensely. A very dramatic illustration of this has been Russian President Vladimir Putin's justification for the invasion of Ukraine in February 2022, in which he invokes the spectre of the Second World War. Speaking at the start of the war, he explains, 'The purpose of this operation is to protect people who for eight years now have been facing humiliation and genocide perpetrated by the Kyiv regime. To this end, we will seek to demilitarize and denazify Ukraine.' This political narrative has been heatedly rejected not only by Ukraine – whose official Twitter accounts of Putin and Adolf Hitler show the two men gazing lovingly into each others' eyes, writing 'This is not a "meme," but our and your reality right now' (Triesman, 2022) – but also by those entrusted with preserving the memory of the Holocaust, such as the US Holocaust Museum who have said Putin 'misrepresented and misappropriated Holocaust history'. But the response of Jewish Ukrainian President Volodymyr Zelensky, aimed partially at a Russian audience, demonstrates that he is aware how much is at stake with this political narrative.

> When Russians are telling about neo-Nazis and they turn to me, I just reply that I have lost my entire family in the war because all of them were exterminated during World War II … How can I be a Nazi? The Ukraine in your news and the Ukraine of real life are two entirely different places. The difference is that the latter is real.

The contestation over this political narrative – the battle for historical memory – has profound consequences and demonstrates the important role that stories play not only in everyday life but also in warfare.

We see in the above examples how a reading of personal narratives can enrich our comprehension of events usually analysed sociopolitically and historically. More generally, throughout this chapter and Chapter 3, you have read about how narrative research can contribute to our understanding of specific important social research questions in specific fields. In the next chapter, we widen this approach to develop a broader discussion of the ways in which work with narratives is proving useful within social research.

CHAPTER 5

The uses of narrative research

As you will have seen from the examples in the last two chapters, narrative research can be very appealing. Researchers, like most people, love stories: the specificities that draw you in, show you new worlds and challenge you to think differently; the commonalities that you can relate to; the emotional intensity; the humour; the differences that you learn from. What, though, in intellectual and practical rather than personal terms, draws us to narrative research? Why would we choose this kind of research to address the questions that interest us?

We have seen some examples of the uses of narrative research in the case studies in Chapters 3 and 4. This chapter examines the usefulness of narrative research more generally.

Sometimes, people do narrative research purely because they are interested in structural issues about language. Often, however, such structural interests are also tied to broader concerns. For narrative researchers are most often concerned with how narratives show us little-known phenomena, tell us about lives, demonstrate cognitive and emotional realities and interrelate with social and cultural worlds. These concerns have contributed very fruitfully to particular social research fields that we discuss in this chapter. In the field of health and illness research, narrative research's contribution lies especially in the realm of practice. In the field of what are called 'sensitive' topics, narrative research contributes to a more complex and processual framing of research and research ethics. In what follows, we consider narrative research's usefulness in this double way, in relation to its general usefulness and in relation to its value in particular fields.

There are many other fields we could have used as examples: education; social work; crime; work and leisure; politics and human rights; social movements; international development; counselling and psychotherapy; media and communication; art; performance; and management and organizational studies, for instance (Boje, 2001; Fleetwood et al., 2019; Meretoja, 2019; Ryan, 2022; White and Epson, 1990). These are fields where we hope you will explore narrative research's contribution yourselves.

A. Finding out about little-known phenomena: Exploring narrative 'voice'

Narrative research, like other qualitative research, is often said to have value because it can shed light on phenomena about which little is known. It is frequently used in an exploratory way to 'illuminate' the life circumstances of individuals and communities – mundane realities that research neglects. In response, Ann Phoenix and her co-authors (2020, for instance, in *Researching Family Narratives*, focus on how families give narrative voice to everyday worlds of, for instance, food – shopping, cooking, meals – and their environments – roads, transport, green spaces.

However, narrative research is also deployed to 'illuminate' more specific circumstances that deepen forms of harm and exclusion. The case study on violence and abuse presented in Chapter 4 is an example. There, we argued that one problem faced by people who experience violence is finding a safe way to give voice to their story, have it heard and legitimized. In what follows, we look at another example of research investigating phenomena about which little is known, in connection with critical reflections on narrative 'voice'.

The following extract comes from an interview with Alan, who participated in research conducted in Scotland to inform health promotion for gay men with Human Immunodeficiency Virus (HIV; Davis and Flowers, 2011; Flowers and Davis, 2013). In the example below, Alan, who has HIV, discusses HIV treatment, its effects and considerations for his HIV-negative partner:

> We found that once we settled well into the relationship, I became very comfortable with the whole kind of HIV thing, and I suppose I, at some stage in that time, decided well it wouldn't be that bad a thing, given today's treatments and you know, today's kind of view of HIV and such like. It wouldn't be that bad a thing if it were to happen. So I took the view that I wasn't going to be this, 'Right we've got to do every last thing properly and not share toothbrushes and be very careful with razors!' ... I just thought 'no, we use razors and if you cut yourself, you know, stick it in the bin or something'. You know, it would just be that. But of course that's not always enough because you don't always see things right? I don't know how many people normally get that off a razor, probably never, [laughter] ... people can be very, you know, would separate everything and the different towels and just do everything, doing condoms for everything and I just took the view that wasn't really a kind of normal way of viewing our relationship ... I suppose kind of sort of settled into this idea, well this might happen at some stage, you know, and I think once I started to take that view, even things like condoms they'd disappear, at least until the point when either of us were going to cum sort of thing. (Alan, aged 30)

This extract can be read as exercising narrative voice in several ways:

1. Alan's extract permits insight into the nuance and mutability of his experience of HIV-positive serostatus. The extract's value depends on seeing it as Alan's perspective on life with HIV: his experiences, words and related meanings. Insight provided by Alan's account is important to the HIV field where biomedical research approaches dominate, particularly since the introduction of effective HIV treatment in the mid-1990s to late 1990s in the global North. Indeed, Alan's account is predicated on this transition when he refers to 'today's treatments and you know, today's kind of view of HIV and such like'. Collecting Alan's account and others like it adds grassroots

voices to what is mainly a biomedicalized and expert-led field in the affluent, global North.
2. The emphasis on domesticity and life with his partner underlines Alan's speaking position. Intimacy and its meanings are axiomatically and complexly said to be both deeply personal and relational. It is perhaps only through the voice of the narrator that we can gain insight into such personal dimensions of experience.
3. The exercise of narrative voice can also establish the means for sociopolitical action. Alan's account works to create such means. It 'gives voice' to life experience, not simply as subject to HIV's history but as an active interpretation of (and questioning of and even resistance to) the complexities of life with HIV. Through narrative voice, Alan is able to establish his HIV identity in the historical context of effective treatments and to reflect on implications for his relationship.

Valuing narrative voice in the ways we have described depends on several assumptions. Key among these are notions of 'possession' and 'authenticity', which assume that the voice of the narrator is their own and that it gives unrivalled access to their lived experience. Such views are supported by the idea that narrators create their own stories and that how a life is imagined has value simply because it depends on the memory and creative storytelling of the individual.

However, it is also possible to question narrative voice, its assumptions and, therefore, its ability to shed light on little-known phenomena. Key critiques include:

1. Romanticization. Researchers may rely on, and be complicit with, the idea that the narrating subject has a special status as the generator of meaning, over and above history and social mores. Such romanticization may lead researchers to overlook the partial qualities of personal experience accounts, for example, omissions due to failures of memory and the possibility of social desirability bias in the research interaction (for further discussion, see Atkinson, 2009).

2. Reinforcing social exclusion. Giving emphasis to the narrative voice of the researched, and in particular that of the hidden and marginal, can have the effect of reinscribing social marginalization. To approach those who may lack autonomy to gather the collection, interpretation and editing of their stories about the effects of power in their lives may have of simply reinforcing their lack of power. However, as we shall see later in this chapter, the bringing together of such life stories can also enable collective action, helping to move subjects from the excluded margins to the centre.

Narrative voice is acted and performed. As we noted in Chapter 2, Section C, and as demonstrated in the social media examples from Chapter 3, Section C, narrative depends on tellers and audiences. Speaking of one's intimate life or relating to others' experiences that are difficult to tell are processes that also depend on the listener. Narrative voice, then, is not altogether singular and simply possessed and given; it is negotiated, performed and, therefore, dialogical.

These critiques, however, can be addressed by making them part of the research. For example, Alan's extract can be addressed for how he positions himself in relation to the implications of HIV treatments for himself and his partner. It can also be read along with other similar and differing narratives and in relation to the more general history of the advent of effective treatments. In this way, research can moderate notions that it uncritically romanticizes narrative voice. Similarly, narrative researchers can address power in the research relationship directly. Chapter 4's case study on violence and abuse is based on the idea that some stories were difficult, perhaps impossible, to tell until shifts in gender politics made it easier for such stories to be aired and addressed. In this way, the case study makes power both a substantive and a methodological problem, reducing the chance that it will reproduce the effects of power on the oppressed.

It is possible, then, to strengthen narrative research by reflecting on criticisms. As we will see in Chapter 6, Section F, this self-critical approach is also relevant for the ethical conduct of research, where concerns such as power in the researcher–researched relationship, and the depiction of narratives, take centre stage.

B. Understanding lives

We have seen how narrative research can be used to explore social experiences about which little is known and how the voice of the narrator can be an important resource. We also explored some of the provisions that apply to the uncritical exercise of the idea of narrative voice. Underlying these provisions are questions to do with the relationship between narrative and lived experience.

Narrative research provides vivid pictures of people's lives. It seems to let us grasp the complexity, multiplicity and contradiction within lives as well as within stories. In the section above, we saw that it could give insight into lives whose representations are few, marginalized and pathologized. This section discusses different perspectives on the relationship between lives and stories.

Although we think of narrative and lives as closely interrelated, narrative researchers often set aside, leave implicit or qualify their relationship. When narrative is, as Plummer (2001) puts it, a 'theme' for narrative researchers, or when, in Elliott's (2005) terms, researchers take a 'constructionist' approach (Chapter 1, Section C), narrative's relationship to lives is displaced from study. This can happen not only when researchers examine structures of personal narratives in literature (Hatavara et al., 2016), film (Anderson, 2010) and social media (Page, 2018) but also when they are studying verbal narrative structures. Labov's (1997) work on event narratives about fights and deaths, for example, is concerned with these narratives' structure rather than their relation to lives. Similarly, social constructionist approaches, arguing that narratives constitute, at least partially, lived experience, may collapse life experience into the stories people tell. But it is clearly important, for instance in the example in the last section, both that Alan can tell a narrative of 'normal' relationships and that narrative impacts positively on his life with his partner.

Approaches focused more on narrative content than structure may also depart from lives, when they look at how their thematic analysis makes sense of experience rather than examining the exact relation of the themes to the narrator's life. For instance, Arthur Frank (2006) has articulated life stories of illness as 'chaos', 'quest' and 'restitution' variations on a general 'strategic' health narrative – emphasizing the agency of the person who constructs their story – but not always the exact relation of their prior lived experience to narrative type.

Other researchers focus explicitly on narratives as resources for knowledge about lives. The previous section, for example, reflects critically on what we can learn about Alan's life, as well as his narratives, from his 'voice' in research. Narrative resources for understanding lives can be personal documents, like Alan's interview, but they may also be public, like the multilingual poetic narratives of East London lives generated by Sonia Quintero that we referred to in Chapter 2, Section C (Lounasmaa et al., 2024; Quintero, n.d.). Dana Kavelina's (2020) film about living through the war in the Donbas region, another example, also, as noted in Chapter 4, Section A, registers the impossibility of making narrative sense of some life events. Indeed, researchers who claim narratives as resources for making sense of lives, as in the case of Alan's interview and Quintero and her colleagues' poetry, rarely assert a direct, full relation between the two.

We might expect that social research, focused on life stories, as in biographical and autobiographical writing, life histories and oral histories, would operate with a clearer, more complete picture of the relationship between narratives and lives. However, that relationship varies, productively, across the field (Caetano and Nico, 2022; Eakin, 2020). In this form of narrative research, major life events are often understood as organized into the logic of, and as giving texture to, the trajectory of a socially defined 'life course'. Written life histories, in particular, are read as revealing the orderly, phased or staged unfolding of the life course. Such research may also search for the intersections of social forces and lived possibilities, as in research on working-class lives undergoing transformation within the life course and generationally (Connell et al., 1993; see also Harrison, 2009). Research on witness narratives, similarly, is highly sensitive to the past, present and future contexts of those narratives, as in Del Tufo and colleagues' (2021) work documenting and archiving African American personal testimonies of the civil rights struggle (Chapter 1, Section E). In these cases, a narrative of a life is never only a direct expression of that life but is also shaped both by spoken and written narrative conventions and by the life's sociality and history.

The apparent lack of clarity about the relation between life and story across much narrative research sometimes seems to relate to the equation of 'life' with a particular understanding of 'experience' as internal, individual consciousness. Narrative research has, as we saw in Chapter 1, Section E, a historical relation, in western countries especially, to Ricoeur's (1984) phenomenology. Here, human subjects' consciousness is the register of experience, which seeks expression in narrative. This approach provides a clear, but currently rarely fully adopted, account of narratives as transmitting individual life experiences into language.

Some narrative researchers work with a related, psychoanalytic understanding of life as 'experience'. In Biographic-Narrative Interpretive Method (BNIM), for example, researchers search systematically for the 'deep structures' – close to but going beyond the Ricoeurian understanding of consciousness – of the personal experience account (Wengraf, 2019). The focus here is on the 'told story' as holding a particular, 'psychological' form of reality: that of 'the person behind the text'. At the same time, BNIM also sees narrative as a window onto the 'lived life''s personal, social and historical realities.

Other psychoanalytically oriented narrative research has a more focused interest in stories as expressions of psychological realities (e.g. Hollway and Jefferson, 2012). Such research suggests that due to repression and other unconscious processes, the narrator may not be wholly in touch with the meanings they convey in their storytelling. The researcher–researched relation, too, may be shaped in ways outside both conscious personal relations and the power effects discussed in Sections C and D in this chapter, since unconscious elements of the interaction may influence what is said and not said. Individual subjectivities thus lie within narratives, and it may take a psychoanalytically oriented listener to discern them.

Such phenomenologically and psychoanalytically influenced narrative research approaches, eliding 'life' and especially 'experience' with internal individual consciousness and unconsciousness, are, as Chapter 1, Section E also pointed out, less common than previously. Contemporary narrative researchers' non-programmatic, pragmatic, social justice-oriented interests put the primacy and universality of individual subjecthood into question and position lives as lived socially, not just individually, and as inflected but not determined by the narrative representations of those lives. Researchers tend to adopt a 'weak' social constructionism or a 'critical' realism. They do not necessarily draw lines between fictional and non-fictional texts (Ryan, 2022). They view 'experience' as personal and social practices – including representational practices like narration – rather than as the internal preserve of individual subjects. This contextualization of lives and experience goes along with a strong recent emphasis, as we saw in Chapter 1, Section E, on narrative as itself always part of its context and as affecting it – for instance, through working towards social justice. We can see this in, for example, Cardinal and colleagues' (2019) co-research on educational violence against indigenous people, carried out by pupils, teachers and parents as well as researchers; addressing lived experience, including the lived experience of narrative inquiry, as a collective process; and working, itself, as a kind of critical pedagogy. Del Tufo and colleagues' (2021) research on testifying and Quintero's research with community-based poetry groups (Lounasmaa et al., 2024 Quintero, n.d.) are similarly focused on life experiences made and narrated socially and on the research's own potential social effects.

When researchers view 'experience' in this way, it means they are seeing narratives are not only expressing but also creating lives. Indeed, when in Chapter 1 we explored Vanessa Nakate's narrative of her visit to northern Kenya, we looked not at how the story related to Nakate's recent life experiences leading up to this public speech but instead at how its empathy-generating elements might create a sense of commonality and solidarity in its various audiences. And when Frank identified distinct 'illness' narratives, he defined them by how they approached the possibility of healing. 'Restitution' narratives address negative health events in ways that can accommodate and perhaps even overcome them (Frank, 1995). 'Chaos' and 'quest' narratives supply different ways of addressing one's life in the context of a health event. Other researchers have examined these healing possibilities of narrative in medical and therapeutic contexts. Narrative, it is argued, complements health care by offering ways of making sense of and through this, living with major life events, such as cancer diagnosis or chronic illness such as diabetes (for a discussion of narrative medicine, see Chapter 6, Section D). Similarly, within narrative therapy and some family systems therapy, narrative is seen as allowing explicit attention to the possible reframing of lives and as enabling the reconstruction and performance of varying identities (Vetere and Dowling, 2005; White and Epson, 1990).

Other narrative researchers focus explicitly on the convergence of narrative forms with sociopolitical lives and change; the following section examines this focus more thoroughly. For example, Francesca Polletta's (2006) work on the stories told among civil rights activists in the 1960s examines the relationship between particular types of stories of racialization and mobilization and changes in the racialized structure of those activist movements.

While we have demonstrated elsewhere that all narratives involve co-creation, some research takes this idea further and invites participants to become active collaborators in framing the questions, presenting the stories and drawing analysis from them. Such work has been done by Squire (Africa et al., 2017) and Lounasmaa (Lounasmaa et al., 2019; Masserano et al., 2021) with refugee participants and students. Here, writing is done through collaborative practices of storytelling and creative writing exercises, which lead to discussions of how and where such texts should be disseminated. The use of different collaborative and co-creative practices in narrative research can help address power relations as well as gaps in the researchers' knowledge about invisible cultural conventions, specific forms of telling and other blind spots. When the research is based on dialogue and collaborative writing and storytelling practices, the participants gain an understanding of academic storytelling practices and the ways in which narratives get translated into research findings. Such collaborations can amplify voices that are usually not heard and provide opportunities to rethink what counts as academic text and what language and structural barriers we put in place when devising such texts.

There are also stories within stories. Accounting for one's life history can lead to narratives of particular events and situations seen as important. Some of this recounting might even take the form of stories of storytelling, as is the case when people speak of having narrated their lives and experiences for others. For example, as noted in relation to the social media examples discussed in Chapter 3, narrators and their interlocutors use technologies, such as Facebook and health information fora, to create and share narratives that mobilize collective and political action (#MeToo, #BlackLivesMatter and #JeSuisCharlie) or to craft new modes of living (Mumsnet.com) their lives and gain comments and advice from others. In this view, social media lives appear to be particularly heavily narrativized.

Polletta's work traces the stories of the lives of social movements. In this approach, narrative researchers address 'stories of life' – stories that are not about anyone's life in particular. For example, they might focus on human lives in general as depicted in literature or in social science, reflecting on the general and the exceptional in the body of 'life stories' and what they, therefore, make possible or proscribe. Such researchers may also focus on the political economy of life stories, such as the way that stories of the self have become broadcast and social media currency and, more particularly, which stories are given value and which are not. In these cases, a narrative itself is examined, in a sense, in terms of its own 'life' (Davis, 2017).

There are many narratives, too, that do not seem to be about human, or any, 'life'. Nakate's story humanized climate emergency; but Nakate could equally have told stories of animals dying, crops and vegetation in decline, rivers drying and water tables falling to convey that emergency. These, too, would have been stories of lives – not just of the human lives connected with them but also of those other material entities not necessarily linked to humans. Actor-network theorists, new materialists and older materialists, too, have emphasized the need for all materialities to be part of a story. Contemporary narrative researchers such as David Herman (2018) have turned to considering the lives of non-human subjects within narratives; Marie-Laure Ryan (2022) has posited the possibilities of narratives without narrators.

Narratives encompassing broad senses of 'living' beyond the human have rooted and long-lasting traditions among, for instance, indigenous peoples, as Eagle Heart (n.d.) emphasizes in her account of 'ice people' who live with and through ice and her 'story about a rock, an animated rock'. Here, too, materiality and spirituality are not separable. Canham (2023: 5), tracing the story/theory of the Mpondo people, describes their stories and knowledge of an intersection of multiple lives – present and ancestral, individual and collective, local and spanning African diasporas, travelling, colonizing and settling, inhabiting hills and mountains, rivers, seas and dreams.

Lastly, there are stories like Canham's and Kavelina's (2020) film about the Donbas, which mark the disjunctions between stories and lives in what cannot be told. Psychoanalytically influenced narrative researchers tend to ascribe such untellability to the workings of the unconscious within narrative. Contemporary narrative research that views experience and narration as related processes of living is more likely to see narrative failures, diversions and omissions as part of those processes than as unconscious traces. Indeed, such research is contingent enough always to recognize the limits of what narratives can do and what we can know about them.

It has been argued, from a variety of theoretical perspectives, that the significance of narrative is not necessarily what is told but rather in its co-construction and performance. These characteristics imply that when someone relates an aspect of their experience to others, there is no guarantee that it will have the effects the narrator intended. In addition, narrative production itself will be experimental and negotiated – an experience, in the first sense of that word – as storytellers feel their way through what it is possible to say in an interview or in other interactional circumstances. The social 'life', then, of the narrative-as-heard or as-read may be as or more important for lives than the 'life story' *per se*.

In this section, we have seen that stories touching on lived experiences can be analysed to tell us about lives in different ways. The substantive content of the stories might be salient for research. Or, the analyst may focus on understanding narratives more contextually, in terms of what happened; in what situation; with what consequences; who was there; the language used to relay the story and how the story was produced. Analysis might also examine how others involved with the research read the story; how each responds to the other's analysis; and what other stories, and storied actions, come out of the research. In much narrative research, lives are understood through an emphasis on one of these processes – through a focus on language and change in the civil rights movement, for example, in Polletta's (2006) case. In other research, like Cardinal and colleagues' (2019) narrative inquiry on pedagogies and indigenous peoples, and Del Tufo and colleagues' (2021) facilitation of civil rights testimonies tying the past, through the present, to the future, all of these processes were in play in the narrative understanding of lives.

C. Understanding narratives in relation to social, cultural and political contexts

What can narratives tell us about the social, political and cultural contexts in which they are constructed and function? As the above section suggests, even the most personal of narratives do not talk only about individuals' internal lives. Some narratives of 'lives' like those we have just discussed give extensive and complex pictures of the social worlds, communities and generations of which they speak. Narrative's function as a resource 'window' onto a particular socio-historical moment, and a way of understanding that moment's meaning for the narrator, is, then, the first formulation of the connection between stories and their wider contexts that we will consider.

Molly Andrews (2017a) argues that individuals tell their stories as members of a historically specific generation. Each generation has a different way of constructing and narrating stories, which reflect 'both the specificity of their location and their position within a wider historical perspective' (Andrews, 2002: 82). Narratives of each generation are constitutive of a consciousness, which enable that generation to come to a deeper understanding of its historical location and to appreciate its ability to work on the social world in which it is constructed (Andrews, 2002: 79–80). There is a close mutual association between narratives and social change in this account, based on the degree to which people identify as part of relatively homogeneous generational groups.

Similarly, we have described the interconnection between narratives and social change in Chapter 4's account of Esin's research on sexual narratives, interconnected with narratives of sociopolitical transformation within the context of Turkish modernity. Referencing a more recent history, Davis and Lohm (2020) analysed the public health, media and personal experience narratives created in response to the 2009/2010 influenza pandemic and documented how the changing course of the pandemic came into public life and, for some, had personal impact. In a later parallel, Masserano and Lounasmaa (2021; Lounasmaa et al., 2024) researched, in collaboration with refugee students, those students' narratives of their experiences of the Covid-19 pandemic, how they differed from other experiences and how they were framed within existing exclusions and marginalizations.

There is also a close and direct connection in many contemporary societies between narratives and social movements, which shifts the relationship between stories and social change from one of association to one of determination. Social movements create the possibility for new stories to emerge and be heard at specific historical moments through the social changes they help to produce. Namiba and colleagues' (2023) collective narrative of new ways of living with HIV, for example, emerged, as they themselves document, from powerful histories of community and coalitional advocacy and activism around this earlier pandemic.

At the same time, narratives of social change are themselves historically and culturally specific constructions which invite and motivate individuals to participate in democratic movements. Storytelling can be a political action that contributes to the development of participatory political cultures, as Plummer (1995, 2001, 2019) states. For example, the telling of intimate stories, such as sexual stories, has created shifts in the ways in which politics are conceptualized and performed in contemporary societies. Movements around identity politics, such as feminism, gay and lesbian civil rights and disability rights movements, and movements against forms of oppression, such as racism, immigration control, sexual harassment and violence against women, would not have flourished if people had not told stories and these stories had not been heard. Earlier written autobiographical narratives, too, have had such effects, as we indicated when considering the history of narrative research in Chapter 1 (see also Tamboukou, 2018).

Plummer (1995), like Polletta (2006), argues that narratives gather people together and potentiate social action, as Nakate's Dorcas story aims to do. We might indeed argue that narrative has an inevitably socio-moral and political, not just social, function because it positions people as social actors who must account for themselves and not just communicate. This argument converges on narrative research from the very different theoretical positions of philosophers like Alasdair MacIntyre (1984), psychologists such as Jerome Bruner (1990) and the social theorist Judith Butler (2005), for whom 'giving an account of oneself' always carries the double meaning of both life narrative and life responsibility. The argument also helps ground the contemporary social justice current within narrative research, described in Chapter 1, Section F.

An understanding of the sociality of narrative leads us, too, to think about smaller-scale narratives as highly social. For many researchers, a self-narrative is always an articulation of self-identity in relation to others (Riessman, 2008). To achieve this articulation, narratives work, often in complex and contradictory ways, by positioning their makers, their other characters and their audiences (Phoenix, 2013) socially as well as personally. Alan's story, told to Davis and Flowers (2011), positions him in relation to an interviewer he clearly thinks will understand his story, but also strongly identifies Alan as a responsible as well as loving partner in the context of the current UK epidemic. In Chapter 4, the stories women told to Esin, in her research on sexualities, position the narrators and often their parents as forward-thinking women and men within a specific Turkish context which the women expect Esin to understand. Dorcas told her story to another young African woman concerned about the climate emergency – but also within a UNICEF clinic, and indirectly, through Nakate's amplification, to a UNICEF audience, and then to a wider public, including many who might not support food aid or 'loss and damage' restitution for countries most affected by climate emergency. Moreover, the story was told at a particular time, when drought-related food insecurity in northern Kenya had become big news. Nakate's speech was a bridge between Dorcas, all climate-emergency-affected northern Kenyans unable to feed their children, and the food-secure minority world that funds UNICEF. But that narrated relationship was also a kind of sisterhood between Dorcas and the young Ugandan woman, positioning Nakate on Dorcas's side, speaking her words with a louder voice, as young people are indeed persistently doing across the world on behalf of their and future generations.

Particular *forms* of stories have a social and historical significance of their own. Part of narrative researchers' interest is, consequently, in what kinds of stories are possible to tell and hear within a specific historical and social context. For instance, the narratives of interpersonal violence analysed by Margareta Hydén, and the coming-out stories referred to in Chapter 1 and this chapter, constitute a whole set of stories that, as Plummer (2019) noted, did not have currency before the second half of the twentieth century.

Another obvious example of a recent narrative type in contemporary western popular culture is the story of personal progress or salvation that you see on many reality TV shows and also hear people telling in everyday lives: the 'it's been a journey' story. Is this a new story or a new form of a very old one – the religious conversion story, perhaps? Does Nakate's Dorcas story belong to this salvational or redemptive narrative (McAdams, 2006) type, also? It seems a little different; it ends with a coda, not about meeting climate goals, or securing UNICEF's therapeutic food programme, but about representing young climate activists 'to those who have the power to bring real change'.

Sometimes, narrative researchers draw on existing literary work on genres to understand social narrative repertoires. For example, Karen Wells (2013) draws on the genre of melodrama to analyse NGO narratives like Nakate's – though she focuses on films rather than speeches. Wells describes how melodrama is limited in its social effects by its homogenization, Eurocentrism and abdication of analysis for affect. But she also points out that melodrama's emotionality generates solidarities, and its moral clarity supports action.

At other times, particularly in working with narratives of illness, researchers develop genre categories directly from their data to elucidate the sociality of narratives. Arthur Frank's (1995/2013) categories of restitution, chaos and quest illness narratives, mentioned in the previous section, constitute an influential analysis of how people fashion biosocial dialogues in the context of illness (see also Kleinman, 1988). More recently and specifically, Squire and De Lemos (2022), examining the narratives of people living with two pandemics – HIV and Covid-19 – draw on the work of Ghassan Hage (2015) and Sara Ahmed (2021) to describe oppositional and alter-critical genres of narrating citizenship against the neglect and normalization of these pandemics – as well as a more provisional, but persistent, narrative 'style' of complaint.

Such social 'genre' accounts of narratives have the advantage of linking people's stories with the wider social and cultural representations with which they live. However, they can apply genre categories simplistically or overgeneralize from their own data. They also tend to ignore particular sociopolitical contexts, such as the campaign moment that made Nakate's story so significant, as opposed to the NGO melodrama genre into which it fits. They may also neglect the personal specificities of narratives, which interest so many narrative researchers.

D. Narrative research's effects on practice: Understanding health and illness

We have, throughout this book, referred to narratives that have had clear effects on the world. Nakate's amplification of Dorcas's and similar stories had an impact on public opinion that can be estimated, albeit crudely, from her narrative's media circulation and citation. Namiba and colleagues' (2023) assemblage of stories of and about African lives with HIV in the UK has already made a community life for itself through its 'roadshow' with HIV organizations across the UK. To explore further the ways in which narratives have effects on practice, we are going to explore here how they impact the field of health and illness.

Narrative concepts and methods are key resources for research on health and illness, and health and illness themselves. To become significantly ill is always more than the disease or accident itself because the event transforms lived experience and may come to shape relationships with others in social worlds. Mobility, employment, healthcare access, parenting and family life are some aspects of social life that can be disrupted by illness. Also, due to illness, identity may be questioned, and life expectations may change radically. Through these effects and transformed meanings, it is possible to say that illness – in contradistinction with disease – *is* narrative. The recurrent and highly popular medical soaps lend support to the significance of this illness-narrative relation. In South Korea, for example, *Hospital Playlist* is the latest among other popular medical dramas which reach audiences across Asia. *Casualty* has been broadcast weekly in the UK since 1986, and *Flying Doctors* commenced in the 1980s in Australia, followed by similar medical dramas in the decades that followed. Moreover, illness narratives need not be fictionalized to attract audiences. Reality medical dramas – *Emergency: NYC* and *24 hours in A&E*, for example – are highly narrativized depictions of health and illness that capture profound life events and move audiences.

Narrative is also present in the relationships that people have with others to help them respond to illness. Talk of symptoms and life events during a medical consultation are disclosure narratives that make diagnosis and treatment possible. Illness narratives can also extend to the stories told by carers and relatives about their lived experiences with those who are ill. These kinds of illness narratives often occur as oral narratives in everyday conversations with family, friends and colleagues. It is important to recognize that illness narratives, as such, do not only exist in, for example, an interview or patient testimonial but are also disseminated in social life and undergo continual retelling.

Scholarship in the field of illness narratives is decidedly transdisciplinary, including physicians, social scientists and humanities scholars, among others. The work of Arthur Kleinman, Arthur Frank, Byron Good, Michael Bury, Elliott Mishler, Anne Hawkins, Corinne Squire, Trish Greenhalgh, Brian Hurwitz and Rita Charon are useful starting points for engaging with the richness of the field. Kleinman's *The Illness Narratives* (Kleinman, 1988) focused on the lived experience of illness and was important for demonstrating that disease and illness are not synonyms. This work revealed that how people interpret suffering and healing is vital to ethical and just healthcare practice.

US literary theorist Anne Hawkins critically examined the burgeoning publishing of biographical and autobiographical accounts of illness and developed the genre notion of pathography. Her book *Reconstructing Illness: Studies in Pathography* (1998) described the genre's significance for counteracting medical paternalism. Online patient testimonials, blogs, social media posts and other materials are richly nuanced pathographic digital media. Researchers have explored the narrative themes in anti-vaccination social media postings to help shape public policy and communications on the Covid-19 vaccine (Amaral et al., 2022).

The medical sociologist Arthur Frank (1995/2013) suggested that interest in illness narrative reflects late modern individualism and the related emphasis on suffering recognized in its individual particularity, echoing pathography. Frank's book, *The Wounded Storyteller* (1995/2013), is part personal reckoning with illness and part elaboration on key illness narrative variations: restitution, chaos and quest. In this regard, illness narrative provides a means for negotiating the, sometimes, profound existential challenges that come with the loss of health.

Kleinman, Hawkins and Frank are by no means the only contributions to the field of illness narrative, but they do show that it can be analysed in different ways and for varying effects. How people narrate the illness experience provides insight into what it means for them and how they seek to contend with the psychosocial burden of disease and its effects. Researchers often employ narrative research, therefore, to help strengthen healthcare practices. They might elicit narratives in an interview, diaries and video, or they may analyse found texts – patient testimonials, social media and letters – for their illness narrative properties. Researchers in either elicited or found narratives research mode may focus on events and symptoms in biographical context. By weaving together the threads of illness events into the fabric of personal lives, physical symptoms are transformed into lived experience, and diagnoses and prognoses attain meaning within the framework of personal biography. These processes are now often acknowledged by many working within the health and illness field, and are viewed by them as part of processes of healing, recovery and survival.

Illness narratives are also powerfully collectivizing. The telling of stories about illness enables other people to comment on the narrative and to offer new interpretations and suggestions. Thus, narratives serve as means for presenting, discussing and negotiating illness and how to relate to it. These dialogues on the meanings of narrative transform individual experience into collective experience. In Alan's HIV narrative, discussed earlier in this chapter, he relates the social unfolding of the impact of the pandemic – first with intimate others, later perhaps with friends and doctors as well as researchers, as in this case – and points to the changing circumstances of this still very uncertain pandemic (Squire, 2013; Grattan, 2019). This kind of collectivizing is often a first and important step in generating health advocacy and activism and is recognized as such by many patient groups and campaigning health organizations.

One of the benefits of narrative approaches to health and illness is their capacity to reveal the interpersonal and affective qualities of lived experience. Illness narratives, as in Alan's example, are often comprised of characters apart from the narrator and have dramaturgical features. Illness narratives can include the diagnostic moment, when the doctor first informed the narrator of their illness, and disclosures, comprised of others who need to be informed and their reactions. These peopled illness narratives provide important insight into the social relations that give meaning to disease and make effective healthcare possible. The narration of events like these can also have a dual affect: they can depict the emotional intensity of these events and move the listener towards their own feelings and experiences. In this way, narration is its own drama and deepens the meaningfulness of the teller-listener relation.

Echoing the ways in which illness narrative has been popularized in public life through medical drama and pathography, illness narrative concepts are increasingly applied in communications and social marketing to shape responses to health. For example, graphic novels have been used to promote awareness of Covid-19 (Kearns and Kearns, 2020). It is assumed that narrative approaches to health communication have advantages over simply transmitting information because the reader is more able to identify with the plights and triumphs of characters in the narrative. The affective qualities of responses to illness can, therefore, be explored in these narratives. Graphic novels and other uses of narrative to shape healthcare practices can also have a folk-tale quality in the sense that they ask the reader to reflect on the fate of characters and, therefore, consider their own practices in light of possible future effects on health. For this reason, narrative ethics have become an important analytical frame for the use of illness narrative to shape health practices (Barret et al., 2022).

In this vein, too, narrative medicine (as previously noted) is sometimes an element of the professional development of medical professionals (Greenhalgh, 2006), helping them to orient to the lived realities of patient experience to improve diagnosis, treatment plans and ongoing care. Illness narrative can be the means by which doctors and other medical professionals can acquire a more detailed clinical picture of the patient. It is through becoming versed in the patient's narratives that it becomes possible for the medical professional not only to make a correct diagnosis but also to propose a treatment programme that is feasible and acceptable to the patient. Becoming acquainted with the patient's illness narratives also plays an important role in determining how the communication between doctor and patient develops and how the patient experiences the information conveyed by the doctor. Medical practitioners' understanding of this requirement for dialogic narrative often appears now in their own involvement with patient groups and, more institutionally, in their integration of patients and patient-led organizations into their treatment procedures.

E. Narrative's effects on practice: Understanding 'sensitive topics' and 'sensitive events'

Narrative researchers typically work hard to create space for research participants to talk about the topic in focus. Without the limitations of too many questions or a preset theoretical frame, the participant is encouraged and supported in order to give his or her view and the researcher is prepared to listen. This makes narrative approaches well-suited for the study of sensitive topics and events.

It is important to emphasize the difference between an *event* that involves sensitive, even traumatic, experiences and a sensitive *topic*. An event is something you experience, and a topic is something that appears in a discussion and is dealt with discursively. An event that involves a traumatic experience has the potential to form a sensitive topic without necessarily doing so. Talk about a traumatic experience, for example, may pose a threat and may re-traumatize the traumatized, but such talk can just as well hold out the possibility of healing.

The relationship between teller and listener is the defining factor for what is a sensitive topic and what is not. It also reflects the cultural situatedness of this relationship. According to prevailing norms in most cultures, sensitive topics, especially if they are also intimate topics, should not be discussed in public or with unknown persons. They can be discussed in intimate relationships such as between a couple, within the family or with a close friend. This type of talk even defines such relationships. Outside of intimate relationships, sensitive topics can be discussed in special relationships using particular discourses that strip the topics of their intimacy, like doctor–patient discourses. The researcher–informant relationship is another example. For the shared aim of gaining knowledge on intimate and potentially sensitive topics, the researcher and informant are in agreement in defining their relationship as one in which sensitive topics can be discussed.

Even if a narrative researcher is trained to create space in which vulnerable interviewees, such as victims of violence, can talk about sensitive events, this is not a straightforward task. As a researcher, you are the one who asks your interviewees for something that is valuable to you, that is, their experiences. Your interviewees are in the dominant position, and you are in the subordinate. However, things are a bit more complex than that. As a researcher, you hold a culturally highly valued position; that might be the reason why people want to talk with you. Despite this esteemed and powerful position, if the potential interviewee does not want to talk with you, you are powerless.

In this sense, the research interview is a complicated power relation that needs to be carefully negotiated in order to serve as a safe space for dealing with sensitive topics. This negotiation needs to be done before the research encounter starts in order to get an informed consent from the potential informant, but it might need to be renegotiated during the course of the research process. It is not always possible to foresee when sensitive topics may emerge.

A narrative approach to your research can serve as the foundation for such negotiations, as for your research project as a whole. As a narrative researcher, you can offer a solid frame for the encounter between yourself and the interviewee, based on a joint interest in what he or she has to tell. You do not equip yourself with a battery of questions that will inexorably interrupt the interviewee and split the story. Your opening question is a variation of one of the inviting questions we all know, 'tell me about it'. This question offers a tangible base for the interview, at the same time as it indicates the existence of two different positions, the interviewee as teller and the interviewer as listener. A narrative approach also includes the researcher's responsibility for the interview situation and preparedness to intervene if the story gets too hard to tell. This responsibility is always important to be aware of, but even more so if the topic for the interview is a sensitive one. Taking a narrative approach thus leads you, as a researcher, to a helpfully complex understanding of the research process and ethics around 'sensitivity'.

A narrative approach to 'sensitive topics' research is, as we can see, capable of dealing with many of the complexities and variabilities that come along with a commitment to such topics. In this chapter, we have looked at this and a number of other productive outcomes that can come about from conducting narrative research. In the chapter that follows, we pay more explicit attention to the difficulties that narrative researchers encounter and how they negotiate the processes of doing narrative research.

CHAPTER 6

Challenges in narrative research

Throughout this book, we have seen that narrative research offers diverse and exciting approaches to social science or social inquiry. In the final chapter, we are going to address some of the challenges of narrative research by focusing, first, on general questions about narrative research and, second, on a summary of 'how-to' issues around narrative research, related to what we have already seen of narrative research in operation. The first section of the chapter leads into the second. We move from issues of how to decide on your narrative research project, how to conduct it, how to do the analysis and convey its results through issues of the ethics of narrative research to broader questions about the truth and value of narrative research.

Many authors before us have reflected on how to pose and answer these questions, and would be helpful to accompany the considerations below – for instance, Boonzaier (2019), Butina (2015), Clandinin and Rosiek (2019), Mishler (1986/1995), and Riessman (2008).

A. Are there instructions for doing narrative research?

There are no strict instructions on how to do narrative research. Depending on the research questions and researchers' interpretation of what narrative is and how it is analysed, a researcher may focus on different aspects of narratives, such as the structure, content, context and performance of narratives. As we have seen in this book, such flexibility has created an extended family of creative approaches to narrative research which utilize a wide range of narrative media as data, such as interviews, letters and visual material and varying analytical methods, and which are grounded in sometimes contradictory, sometimes closely related theoretical perspectives.

As in other social science research, there are basic research steps that provide the researcher with a coherent framework to design and conduct their research. These are:

1. situating the theoretical approach,
2. selecting the analytical strategy,
3. collecting or co-constructing data to be analysed,
4. selecting or preparing narratives to be analysed,
5. analysing narratives.

We have already talked about many of these steps. Here, we sketch the procedure for each of them.

1. Situating the theoretical approach

As mentioned in Chapter 1, in western social science, there are often said to be two key approaches to narrative research: one which naturalistically, in Elliott's (2005) terms, takes narratives as resources and which is close to positivism, realism and empiricism; and the constructionist approach – allied to interpretivism – within which narrative itself is a topic. The approaches also differ from each other in the way they approach narrative analysis. While naturalist approaches understand narratives as a medium to analyse the lives of storytellers, constructionist approaches analyse narratives as means of social construction. Of course, we can try to treat narratives in both these ways. Many researchers do precisely this. And as we have seen, modified constructionism or naturalism are common approaches.

It is helpful to try to clarify theoretical positions before doing research. For we make research-related decisions from these positions, which we occupy even if we are not aware of them. For example, if we are interested in the life histories of a group of people who are members of a particular generation because we want to tell the history of that generation, then our research could be situated within a 'naturalist' approach that assumes a transparency between life histories and history. If we are interested in the connections between narrative performances and identity construction among young people, we would be more likely to position life history research within a 'constructionist' approach.

It's important to remember, though, as explored in Chapter 1, Section G, that these divisions are currently often blurred within the practice of narrative research and also that many of the philosophical underpinnings of the divisions have specific and oppressive histories and presents. Conventions around ontology and epistemology, therefore, need to be addressed critically by challenging them directly and by generating alternatives. We could, for instance, draw on Tuhiwai Smith's (1999) chapter on 'twenty-five indigenous projects', which documents dialogic processes between existing and indigenous understandings of 'research'. Many such processes – such as testimonies, storytelling, remembering, revitalizing and connecting – are close to narrative research and practice.

2. Selecting the analytical straterty

How stories are analysed is an important component of narrative research. We have discussed examples of different approaches to narrative analysis in Chapters 1, 3 and 4. Depending on the aspects of narratives which they deal with, we can categorize these approaches under three categories: Analysis focusing on structure, analysis focusing on content and analysis focusing on contexts in which narratives are produced and consumed. There is no predefined best way to do narrative analysis. Narrative researchers need to be open to what narratives themselves offer to researchers, and to pursue their own approaches. For example, the research examples we discussed in Chapters 3 and 4 analyse the content of narratives to a certain extent, while at the same time analysing the sociocultural (as in internet-related research, research on sexual narratives) and emotional (as in research on abuse and violence) contexts in which the personal narratives under analysis are constructed, in relation to other kinds of narratives.

Returning to the frequent contemporary framing of narrative research as oriented towards social justice, Boonzaier (2019) suggests we follow several different analytic 'phases'. These phases enable her to pay attention to the marginalized and disempowered position of the South African sex workers with whom she worked and also to recognize their strategies of resistance. Boonziaer starts from a content-based narrative thematic analysis; moves to a more 'contextual' decolonial, intersectional analysis; and then reads against the grain of apparent 'content', again more contextually, to elucidate narratives of resistance. But such a synergistic building-up of material and political as well as representational analysis cannot really be reduced to 'structural', 'content' and 'context'-based analytic approaches.

3. Collecting or co-constructing data to be analysed

As we discussed in the section on 'where to find narratives' (Chapter 1, Section D), narratives can be discovered in many different places. Research interviews are usually where narratives are elicited in social science research, but interviews are not the only source. Researchers may look for narratives in materials that are written (books, letters, diaries, shopping lists, CVs), visual (photos, still images) and audiovisual (videos, films, social media posts) as well as other discursive spaces such as everyday conversations or internet exchanges, patterns of everyday activity and the networks of meaning that collect around objects like clothes, souvenirs and meals, that are important in people's lives.

Engaging in research with people living with cognitive and/or linguistic disabilities often can make storytelling challenging. One way to facilitate storytelling is to provide support in the interview situations. Sometimes, a significant other or the interviewer can engage in gentle support in, for instance, finding words or names or reminding them about where in the story they are. The support must not take over the storytelling from the interviewee but rather function as a scaffold supporting the interviewee to continue the storytelling. Using photos or pictures may also support storytelling by evoking memories or by reminding the interviewee about the topic of the interview and story (Hydén, 2018a).

We have discussed throughout this book the increasing tendency of narrative researchers to work alongside participants or to erase or redraw boundaries between 'researcher' and 'participant'. This tendency means that the type of material gathered, and the means of gathering it, may be decided by a dialogue between researchers and participants or by participants themselves. In Esin's (2017) work with young people making art in East London, for instance, the type of visual art generated, and the materials used to generate it, was generally determined by participants. Luttrell's (2020) long-term photographic work with young people largely followed their own tempos and schedules. Carver (2021) describes a necessarily very high level responsiveness to participants' lives and preferences in her research process and questions. Abdi (2023) entered into an extended conversation with the young men who were her participants about research process and modalities.

4. Selecting or preparing narratives to be analysed

Selecting and preparing narratives for analysis is an important part of the analytical process. Both processes are related to the analytical approach you choose. For example, in the research on sexual narratives, considered in Chapter 4, Esin took the whole interview as the analytical unit, as a narrative of self and sexuality, and she transcribed all the interviews with the same level of detail. However, she selected particular excerpts to focus on in her analysis, in order to exemplify patterns seen throughout the interview and to explore in detail interviewees' positioning strategies. Some narrative researchers interested in positioning might go further and prepare much more detailed transcripts of exemplary speech segments for their analyses.

Rather differently, Davis and Lohm (2020) treated their interview and focus group material on pandemic influenza as the 'database' and looked for common and divergent story patterns across the materials, as did Harrison when dealing with her interviews on the place of photography in people's lives. In such work, the excerpts presented in conference papers and journal articles tend to be the clearest and most typical examples of narrative categories. That is, they represent a large number of other narratives, similarly identified and analysed.

5. Analysing narratives

There are some general questions which narrative researchers respond to while analysing stories, which relate loosely to the ideas of narrative structure, content and context considered above. Sometimes, the process of posing and responding to questions is done explicitly, sometimes not. We have tried during the book to make the process explicit because we think that approaching narrative analysis in a planned and thoughtful way is a good route to fuller and deeper analyses, which also allow for more engagement with research participants and with other researchers.

The answers to the questions about analysis differ, depending on the researcher's field as well as theoretical and methodological questions. These are as follows:

1. *How are the stories structured?* You will have seen that many of the stories we have looked at can be considered in this way. For instance, the very first story that we started with, Nakate's amplification of Dorcas's story, moves from her recounting of this individual emergency to the much larger emergency of which it is a part and then to possible NGO and broader solutions. The stories told by Esin's female Turkish research participants alternate between adherence and resistance to the dominant cultural narrative of a modern Turkish woman's life. The stories of domestic violence told by M. Hydén's informants made sense only if we read them as structured by the agency, as well as the suffering, of women and children.

2. *What are the content categories or themes that the stories focus on?* Much of the work that we have examined throughout this book addresses narratives in this way. Chapters 3 and 4 present many examples, particularly in the sections on internet narratives and political narratives.

3. *Who produced the stories, and by what means (e.g. discursive, performative) are stories constructed?* M. Hydén's research on responses to abuse, Harrison's (2002) research on family photos and Andrews's work on political narrative are good examples within this book (Chapters 3 and 4) of how such questions can be addressed.
4. *How are stories produced, and how do they work in specific socio-historical contexts?* Plummer's (1995) research on sexual stories and Esin's work (Chapter 4) provide useful examples here.
5. *How are stories silenced and/or contested?* Riessman's (1993) research on fertility and Squire's (2007, 2013a) research on narratives of human immunodeficiency virus (HIV) are interesting examples within the narrative research literature. L. C. Hydén's, M. Hydén's and Esin's work in this book (Chapters 3 and 4) are also good illustrations.

We want now to move on to some of the challenges that you may face when narrative material seems particularly difficult to deal with analytically.

B. How can I deal with 'difficult' narrative materials?

When people construct stories of themselves and others, their stories do not provide us with unmediated meanings. As we have seen, researchers, as well as participants, become part of a mediation process through co-constructing and interpreting narratives. This gives researchers a responsibility beyond consent and confidentiality while working with narratives. However, this must not mean that researchers should shy away from researching difficult and sensitive topics, as this would entail avoiding social and political responsibility as a researcher.

For example, what we investigate in our research may have potentially threatening effects for participants when the participants' private experiences are under investigation and when the research is concerned with social control. Similarly, telling about their personal experiences of politics and oppression may have dangerous consequences for research participants who live in strict, anti-democratic political regimes or in conflict areas. Of course, topics and stories regarded as private and/or dangerous vary culturally and situationally, and this variation itself poses dilemmas for both participants and researchers.

In narrative research, there are blurred lines between what is said and unsaid, what is heard and not heard and what is analysed and not analysed. Researchers need to be very attentive listeners in all phases of research and be careful not to cross these lines in ways that research participants do not know or want. Margareta Hydén's research on responses to abuse in Chapter 4 provides a good example of the need for sensitive researcher positioning. Stories of abuse are often stories which people do not want to tell but which have to be told. There is a fine distinction between listening to these stories and interfering in individuals' lives with an authoritative voice to tell them to take the 'right' action to stop the abuse. An attentive listening process enabled Hydén to understand the complexity of abuse cases in which there is no one 'right' position or action.

The integration of critical, systematic reflexivity into narrative analysis is a way for researchers to deal with difficult material (see Chapter 2, Section D). Reflexivity as a part of research practice means examining all research decisions: theoretical assumptions, selection of participants and/or material to analyse, interviewing/co-constructing data, analysing the data and presenting the analysis. Reflexivity also includes the deconstruction of power relations within and beyond the research, not only those involving the more or less powerful position of the researcher but also those involving the social characteristics of the researcher and the researched. As we have discussed in Chapter 2, reflexivity is closely related to research ethics. It is considered as a political practice in certain research contexts, such as in feminist research. There is a long line of feminist arguments about reflexivity and the necessity of the systematic problematization of power relations between researchers, participants and audiences (Stanley, 1995).

People living with a communicative disability often tell stories that do not necessarily conform to the conventional expectations of how a narrative should sound and look. As researchers, we often tend to conceive and analyse stories told in interviews or identified in observational data, as if they were written. That is, we often expect a beginning, middle and end. Further, we often expect that the *meaning* of the narrative can be found *in* the narrative text and that the narrative primarily is a *representation* of events in the past.

The expectation and hope of eliciting, finding and collecting stories that conform to the literary norms are confounded as storytellers living with communicative disabilities rarely adhere to our conventional narrative expectations. These disabilities are connected to, for instance, cognitive and linguistic challenges resulting from neurocognitive or neurodevelopmental disorders or acquired brain injuries. Rather than telling well-organized stories in interviews or in clinical or everyday settings, those with communicative disabilities quite often tend to upset the narrative norms that researchers implicitly assume (Hydén, 2018b).

In analyzing these kinds of stories, it is often important for us as researchers to be on the outlook for what may seem sense-less or absurd. What may appear as 'sense-less' and 'absurd' could perhaps better be seen as a poetic rendering of experiences or as something that, while it falls outside the existing framework of research understanding, may nevertheless be a significant aspect of the research. As researchers, we may want to engage in mutual meaning-making through listening and understanding in new and often surprising ways, especially to find out what might be salvaged beyond the pure verbal utterance.

C. Can I combine different kinds of data and analysis?

One of narrative research's strengths is that it provides ways of working across different kinds of materials and allows for different ways of analysing them. Narrative researchers choose materials of many kinds. Common strategies include interviewing, sampling online materials and gathering examples of naturally occurring speech, letters and diaries, photographs and video. Also figuring among narrative research materials are public and private documents (birth certificates, newspaper reports, greetings cards, scrapbooks), court reports, literary works, drama, representational and abstract artwork, dance, music, souvenirs and mementoes, buildings and landscapes and ethnographic records of patterns of action within everyday lives.

Some researchers might choose to work with different kinds of narrative materials in combination. In their research on pandemics, Davis and Lohm (2020) considered the ways in which the well-understood and long-standing pandemic narrative was retold at the time of the 2009 influenza outbreak in newspapers, by public health experts, in public health communications and in the personal experience narratives of members of the general public. Davis and Lohm analysed interviews, newspaper articles and public health materials for the interpretation and reworking of canonical pandemic narrative and its application to the social, medical and political conditions of the influenza pandemic in 2009. Analysing these materials together helped to shed light on the psychosocial impact of the pandemic and its unequal effects on different lives, therefore, helping to inform policy and communications on pandemics and similar public health threats.

Choosing whether and how to combine narrative materials depends on where it is assumed narratives can be found (see Chapter 1, Section D). Narratives can be found by the researcher, elicited by them or used in combination. Also, narrative co-construction implies that the researcher and narrator are not necessarily separate in the narrative analysis process (Carver, 2021). The researcher and narrator interact to construct narratives, and at times, the researcher is also a narrator of a kind and vice versa. For example, ethnographic researchers commonly combine their observations with interview materials, both of which can be analysed narratively. Graffy et al. (2019) went further in their narrative-oriented ethnography of homelessness in the United States and combined observations, interviews, meeting minutes and public reports. The ethnographic standpoint also implies that found narratives – media, literature, songs, for example – can be incorporated into narrative analysis. Social media researchers blend analysis of found materials from online sources with elicited narratives. Taylor Annabell (2022) interviewed young women about their social media experiences, incorporating within-interview narration of their Instagram profiles. Co-design researchers work with stakeholders to generate narrative analysis of life situations, at times by co-analysing previously collected interview fragments, as did Clark et al. (2022), who worked with high school students to co-analyse experiential interviews. These approaches apply narrative analysis substantively, dialogically and collaboratively. Substantively, the research is oriented towards the content and shape of the stories constructed in social media and in interviews. Dialogically, different materials are analysed together for what they say about each other and how they combine to reflect cultural patterns. Collaboratively, researchers/participants generate new ways of storying lived experiences, often with the object of the transformation of power relations.

This diversity in the selection, combination and analysis of narratives does not mean that anything goes, that any combination of narrative sources is automatically useful and interesting. The choices made regarding narratives and how to analyse them remain dependent on the question guiding the research activity. The researcher might want to inquire into narrative because they are interested in it for its own sake, and the materials and analysis choices they make might be seemingly disparate. Such choices, however, will be predicated on their interest, that is, on how they have described and problematized narrative. Labov's psycholinguistic work on narratives, for example, addresses narratives across a number of domains such as fights, life-threatening events, the South African Truth and Reconciliation Commission and stories of the deaths of close relations, but it is always interested in how memories of striking events are turned into effective stories with a common form. Others might want to address a very specific research problem through narrative, as is often done in research on social phenomena. In these cases, the choices made will be consistent with what it is the researchers are seeking to achieve in addressing the specific research problem. For example, Squire (2007) focused particularly on the interrelations between popular cultural, social and personal narratives of HIV in her research on the major South African HIV epidemic of the early 2000s rather than simply on research participants' personal stories because of the difficulty at that time, and in that context, in talking publicly about HIV, and the multiple, contested narratives in play around the South African epidemic.

D. How can I write about or otherwise communicate my narrative research findings for a range of research users?

It can be challenging to write about and present your narrative research. The stories that people make of their lives are often so compelling, the findings from one's analysis so complex, that it can be hard to decide how to edit stories, story extracts and analyses, so that they fit into the word limit and textual discipline of a journal article, book or conference paper. Such limits force researchers to decide how most effectively to present their work to an audience. These decisions take in issues about the ways in which it is best to demonstrate and substantiate researchers' arguments. They also shade into aesthetic questions of how to present the story to best advantage and into ethical considerations of how someone's story, edited and contextualized, might be interpreted by others. A related concern can be balancing the presentation of data, such as interview talk, textual materials or images, with their interpretation. Too much data or material, and the research narrative will literally have to speak for itself; this is difficult since the reader may not share your interpretation. Too little data, and the research material may be lost in the discourse of the researcher, possibly reducing the account's credibility and its closeness to the research itself.

Unfortunately, there are no prescriptive solutions to these communication problems. Consistent with how we have portrayed narrative in other parts of this book, narrative researchers vary in how they present their analyses of the narratives they are interested in. Interview-based narrative researchers tend to provide fewer, longer pieces of talk and text than other qualitative researchers, though there are examples of effective accounts of narrative research that contain short extracts from interviews. In research with people with HIV in the UK about the Covid-19 pandemic, Squire and De Lemos (2022) used relatively short interview extracts, discussed alongside each other, to explore how participants' stories resisted dominant narratives of Covid-19. Later, some participants chose to write blogs to develop and make public their own accounts.

Jasmina Sermijn, writing about her narrative interviews with people with mental health problems and the difficulties of negotiating between participant, researcher and research supervisor voices, wrote and published a play to demonstrate the dialogue of these voices (Sermijn et al., 2010). Getting well away from the confines of the journal article or book, Sheila Cavanagh wrote and also staged a play based on lesbian, gay, bisexual, transgender and intersex stories of public and domestic toilets. These stories revealed toilets to be queer spaces/practices found at the intersection of embodiment, gender, sexuality and hygiene (see: https://vimeo.com/88267369). The script reproduced interview extracts and historical documents but had its full research incarnation as a theatre performance, now archived in film form.

In addition, online database technologies, hyperlinking and multimedia interfaces present opportunities for presenting intact and searchable interview data, documents, images and video. Websites developed in this way allow browsers to read transcripts and view videos of interviews, wholly or in segments, organized into themes (see: https://healthtalk.org/ and http://livingstories.org.uk/). Such approaches are often justified in terms of narrative voice: that is, access to the whole interview coupled with video is said to get the reader closer to lived realities (see Chapter 5, Section A, for a discussion of narrative voice).

Relatedly, internet-based narrative communication connects with the notion that reading or viewing someone else's story can bolster social solidarity, have political effects or be therapeutic (see Chapter 5, Section D, for a discussion of narrative's social effects). Non-researchers are already using social media like this, as they share personal testimonials, publish creative works, organize politically and provide support through blogs. So, it makes sense to take account of narrative research online where their social effects may be enhanced. However, like narrative researchers preparing a journal article, book or conference paper, those using internet technologies face choices with regard to which data to present and how to contextualize them. Like print, internet-based communication is similarly edited and contextualized and, therefore, not free of questions of scientificity, aesthetics and ethics.

As was noted in connection with combining a variety of narrative forms in research (see Section C in this chapter), perhaps the best rubric for presenting narrative research is 'do what needs to be done to construct a viable, robust and persuasive research story'.

One of the forms of research communication to which narrative researchers are increasingly paying attention is communication with research participants themselves, not just while obtaining research materials but well before fieldwork commences, during and after the analysis and writing up, and through later feedback (see, for instance, Esin, 2017; Carver, 2021).

E. What is the best way of feeding back research findings to participants?

People volunteer for research for many reasons. Sometimes, they get money or another concrete reward for participating; or they may want to please powerful research gatekeepers. They may participate because they sympathize with the researcher's aims; they see value in the research topic; they wish to assist others; they want to tell their story to a sympathetic listener; or they are keen for 'their story' to be heard by that listener, or more broadly. These motivations imply that participants often invest something of themselves in research and may, therefore, want to know its outcomes. Partly for this reason, as well as to meet their own epistemological and practical goals (for instance, to allow for other interpretive voices or commentary and to provide research results in a form that can directly impact participants' lives), researchers take steps to feed back their findings to participants, acknowledging their contribution and 'giving back'. These include:

1. preparing a plain language 'digest' of the research findings for publication in a practitioner journal or a popular publication;
2. maintaining a website to publish conference papers and short reports on the research's progress;
3. conducting a workshop with participants where findings from the research are presented and discussed;

4. providing participants with a transcript of their interview and discussing it with them;
5. returning to participants after a period of time (in some instances, decades) and asking them to reflect on their lives since the first meeting;
6. holding an informal meeting where participants and researchers can interact, chat about the research and 'close' the project.

How research findings should be fed back is an area for negotiation. The funder of the research and the research community usually expect publications in high-ranked journals and/or widely-read reports. The participants might not find that sufficient. The options suggested above all work best when they are chosen by participants in dialogue with researchers. All these ways of feeding research back are possible; which is chosen is up for negotiation.

Problems can occur when feeding back research results that are connected to the power and status of knowledge in general and academically produced knowledge especially. Your research participants might not like the results and might think those results have the power to influence their lives in unfortunate ways if they are published. Of course, participants are anonymous, but they may still dislike your final product. Or they may react in the opposite way, finding what seems, to you as a researcher, too much hope in the capacity of the research to change their lives for the better. Both these expectations tend to exaggerate the powers of academic research. Most research projects do not reach the level of benefiting or harming people directly by themselves. Their social impacts are small; there are usually many other more influential factors in play. However, narrative research's tendency to involve participants strongly through the extended and intense stories that they tell can mean that their sense of involvement with the research is powerful, and researchers need to address this involvement carefully.

These questions about the engagement of participants in the aftermath of the research also direct our attention to some broader issues about ethics in research, to which narrative researchers, with their often strong and sometimes long-term involvements with their participants, have paid particular attention.

F. How can I do ethical narrative research?

In Chapters 4 and 5, we saw how narrative research is an approach which is particularly well suited to representing the views of marginalized members of society, to 'giving voice to the voiceless' and to exploring under-researched social phenomena. However, as already alluded to, this characterization is not without its critics. Sometimes, narratives of or about the previously hidden or powerless can, rather than challenging the status quo, reinforce social exclusion. In this section, we will look more closely at ethical complexities such as these, which can arise in narrative research.

By the late twentieth century, there was a widespread sense among many social scientists that questions of ethics were far more complicated than indicated on ethics forms provided by institutional review boards. Three decades ago, Zygmunt Bauman published *Postmodern Ethics*, whose key arguments are summarized thus:

> The contemporary ethical position must recognize ambivalence, non-rationality, the aporetic, the non-univeralizable, and the irrational ... contradictions and tensions cannot be overcome, they have to be lived with in struggle and disagreement. (Plummer, 2001: 229)

A significant change has not happened, though, as generally institutions continue to regard ethical review as something which happens primarily before research commences, and Bauman's argument has been taken up by others: 'Ethical research practice is an unfolding process that requires ongoing thought and attention, not something that is fully accomplished by successful passage through the formal process of ethical review, important as this may be' (Goodwin et al., 2020: 36).

Many people who go into the field regard the old rules of conduct as inadequate. Recognizing that researchers not only document 'life out there' but that they critically help to construct knowledge, and indeed what is deemed knowledgeable, some scholars came to feel increasingly uncomfortable about their role in documenting the lives of others. While questions of ethics should always be at the forefront of any research undertaking, it is perhaps the case that for narrative research, the issues are more immediately apparent. For narrative research, which involves documenting stories of individuals and communities, some questions immediately arise:

1. Which stories do we tell?
2. Who is included? Who is excluded?
3. How do we interpret, and then represent, the words and lifeworlds of others?
4. Must our understanding of someone's life correspond with their understanding of their life? If they differ, what is the most responsible thing for us to do? Do our intellectual and ethical responsibilities pull us in different directions?
5. Should we share our 'findings' with our research participants? In what circumstances would it not be desirable to do so?
6. What is the effect of our probing presence?
7. How universal are ethics?

Another ethical question involves what Romm (2020: 29) refers to as 'relational sampling', which is 'explicitly performatively directed, [and] is guided by the ethical concern to propagate relationally directed ways of knowing and living'. In contrast to advocating more distance from research participants and communities in order to maximize objectivity, here, Romm adopts an approach which is similar to the work of many Indigenous scholars, extending the 'possibilities for strengthening our connectivity with 'all that exists'' (Romm, 2020: 30).

Clearly, different kinds of narrative research are more closely associated with different ethical questions. For instance, in visual narrative research, questions of anonymity, informed consent and confidentiality pose different challenges to text-based research. Projects such as Luttrell's Collaborative Seeing Studio (https://collaborativeseeingstudio.commons.gc.cuny.edu/) offer a creative and ethically informed response, embracing 'different ways of seeing, listening to, feeling, re-representing, re-arranging and re-purposing images to engage in research and communicate with what we have learned'. This methodological and ethical approach underlies Luttrell's longitudinal visual narrative research with children

(Luttrell, 2020). While the field of visual narrative expands, there is ongoing discussion and debate regarding what ethical practice is and should be.

Because ethics is such a vital concern for all researchers, we can only advise readers to immerse themselves as thoroughly as possible in the emerging literature which grapples with some of these issues. Although traditionally researchers did not publish about their ethical concerns, this has begun to change. Increasingly, researchers have returned from the field realizing that they were not prepared to grapple with the complexity of the ethical dilemmas with which they were confronted. The narrative scholar who is most likely to conduct ethically sensitive research is the person who realizes the fraught terrain across which they travel and yet who knows that it is possible to move forward, with caution, humility and sensitivity. Tolich and Tumilty (2020: 27) say that the watchword of ethically informed research should be 'Expect the unexpected'. They argue for an 'ethics praxis', which is 'distinct from the simplicity of formal ethics review' and operates on the premise of 'the need for agile and responsive ethics praxis in their work' (Tolich and Tumilty, 2020: 16).

One example of conducting research in 'unexpected' circumstances is that of the Covid-19 pandemic, which posed a number of ethical dilemmas that researchers had not anticipated. Because research carried out at this time was, by necessity, online, there needed to be 'measures to address core ethical challenges around informed consent, privacy and confidentiality, compensation, online access to research participation, and access to resources during a pandemic' (Newman et al., 2021). Newman et al. argue that 'online methods require thoughtful, reflexive, and deliberative approaches in order to identify and mitigate potential and dynamically evolving risks' (Newman et al., 2021: 1).

Questions of ethical narrative research – particularly on sensitive subjects – involve not only the well-being of the participants and communities who are the focus of the investigation but also researchers (Shaw et al., 2020) and transcribers (Hennessy, 2022) who might be vulnerable and 'can potentially experience emotional distress and vicarious trauma' (Hennessy, 2022: 1197).

There is substantial and growing narrative scholarship that investigates ethical questions of research which is not necessarily carried out in the field. Meretoja's (2018: 1) *The Ethics of*

Storytelling: Narrative Hermeneutics, History, and the Possible delves into 'the ethical significance of narrative for human existence', which, she argues, 'has gained unprecedented urgency and intensity'. *Storytelling and Ethics: Literature, Visual Arts and the Power of Narrative* (Meretoja and Davis, 2018: 9) probes the 'ethical potential and limits of narrative', and *The Uses and Abuses of Stories* (Meretoja and Freeman, 2023) explores, among other things, the strategic ways in which stories can sometimes be manipulated to advance unethical outcomes.

G. What is narratives' relation to truth?

A question which is often posed to narrative researchers is how does one evaluate if a narrative with which they are being presented is actually true. At first glance, this is a hard question to answer for several reasons. First, what does 'truth' actually mean as it is applied to the description of human experience? And second, does it really matter? Finally, related to these two questions, there is the question: how much truth is 'true enough'? Let us take these in turn.

1. At the simplest level, when people ask about the truthfulness of an account, they want to know if it really happened. But even as one asks these questions, it immediately begins to unravel. Any two people observing the same phenomena will offer different accounts of their experience. One will emphasize one aspect, while the other might focus on something entirely different. Neither account is false, but each account is and can only ever be partial. There is, as Thomas Nagel has famously asserted, no view from nowhere. That means even with the best of intentions, people will only ever be able to see what is within the boundaries of that which they are able and willing to take in. Those boundaries are porous, forever shifting not only between people but also within the same person. Perspectives are always situated in particular locations, and the closest a researcher can come to uncovering truth is to take full account of not only the

positioning of others but critically of themselves as well. In this way, knowledge is regarded as being constructed and is always and can only ever be partial. Questions surrounding the meaning of truth and multiple truths surfaced in the news when, two days after Donald Trump's inauguration, then US Counselor to the President Kellyanne Conway referred to the existence of 'alternative facts' thereby seemingly implying that the number of people who attended the inauguration in 2017 could, simultaneously, both be more and less than the numbers which attended that of Barack Obama in 2008 and 2012. This claim provoked public outrage and initiated a presidential term, which many came to characterize as 'post-truth' (*The Washington Post* Fact Tracker found that Donald Trump made 30,573 false or misleading claims while in office.).

2. Does it really matter? Well, here, the answer depends on the purpose for which the account is being gathered. If a criminal activity has occurred, it would be glib indeed to say that objective, verifiable truth did not matter. Of course it does, and the moral workings of society – as represented, for instance, by courtroom debate on the proof of evidence – are built upon this premise. On the other hand, much narrative research does not have as its purpose the documentation of an objective truth – there are other approaches to research which are probably better suited to this. Rather, narrative accounts provide an especially rich insight into subjective truths, the frameworks of meaning by which individuals live their lives. If one wishes to understand the 'truth' of how the world appears in the mindset of another, this is an especially adept tool for this exploration.

A corollary of these two points is that narrative truth is not an absolute. Rather there are accounts which are more or less truthful, which correspond to greater or lesser degrees to events which verifiably did happen. But even 'truthful' accounts are fictionalized – in the identification and creation of characters and plot, for instance – and fictional accounts might well reveal a fundamental truth or truths. That remembering is as much a collective as an individual endeavor is a well-rehearsed argument; thus, even while individual accounts may not be objectively true, they may nonetheless resonate with the collective memory. The debate surrounding the discovery of the fictional basis of Benjamin Wilkomirski's supposedly first-hand account of growing up as a Jew during the Holocaust *Fragments: Memories of a Childhood (1939–1948)* testifies not only to the truth of fiction but also to the level of investment we place in being told the truth. At the same time, not all truth claims are equally subject to debate. Ken Plummer comments that these days truth sometimes can seem 'slippery, malleable, unstable' (Plummer 2019: 121), and this represents a wider moral crisis. He then quotes the words of Deborah Lipstadt in the film *Denial*:

> Not all opinions are equal. And some things happened, just like we say they do. Slavery happened, the Black Death happened. The Earth is round, the ice caps are melting, and Elvis is not alive. (Cited in Plummer, 2019: 119)

Distinguishing between what kinds of truth, or truths, one is claiming, for whom, in what context and why are all critical questions when evaluating the 'truthfulness' of a narrative. This is an issue that has become more critical as large language models and visual AI have become capable of better 'deepfake' narratives. While the technological registers involved with such truth simulacra are or seem new, it's important to remember that narratives have probably always been suspended within matrices of truth questions, which are, very often, also questions about the power to author, shape, understand, propagate or question and act on those narratives.

We have, therefore, also argued in this book that while narratives, like other kinds of symbol systems and narrative research itself, are shaped by different, conflicting perspectives, they are not relativistic expressions and creations of multiple truths. Rather, they act as forms of knowledge, sometimes of dominant, sometimes of ignored or repressed kinds, concerning either normative or marginalized and suppressed phenomena. Through narrative research's relational processes of studying narratives, reaching from narratives' internal structures, through their manifest contents, to the multi-levelled contexts of power relations that support them, that research can build and amplify narrative knowledge.

Although this is a book concerned primarily with the methods, with the 'how to' of narrative research, we hope you have also taken from reading it a sense of how connected this question is with the broader questions of how and why to do narrative research, and research in general. We have tried to introduce you to some of the assemblage of narrative research practices within social research. We have pointed out the value of research knowledge, understanding and impact that comes from a field that is in debate with itself, always troubling the very categories that seem to define it. And we have, we hope, shown you that to make these debates part of your own research practice, to find and define your own mode of practising narrative research is an exciting and rewarding way to do research.

FURTHER READINGS AND RESOURCES

Here we provide an annotated set of suggestions for your further reading and viewing, in print and online. These suggestions encompass sources that are important for us as narrative researchers today, as well as others that have historical importance. This is just a short list, but after exploring it, you will also be able to follow up in more detail particular lines of narrative research that interest you.

Abdi, M. (2023). *Somali Students' School Experiences*. London: Palgrave.

An innovative UK study using a decolonial lens to address narrative research.

Andrews, M. (2007). *Shaping History: Narratives of Political Change*. Cambridge: Cambridge University Press.

This book contains chapters on studies conducted in the United States, East Germany, Britain and South Africa and focuses on the relationship between micro- and macro-narratives in contexts of acute political change.

Andrews, M. (2014). *Narrative Imagination and Everyday Life*. New York: Oxford University Press.

This book explores the relationship between narratives and imagination, between what is told and untold, and examines how temporality affects meaning-making over time.

Andrews, M., C. Squire and M. Tamboukou (2013). *Doing Narrative Research*, 2nd edn. London: Sage.

This is the expanded second edition of a much-used introductory text, covering different research methods and varying narrative media and modalities.

Bamberg, M., and M. Andrews (co-editors) (2004). *Considering Counter-Narratives: Narration and Resistance*. Amsterdam: John Benjamins.

This collection contains six early articles on this topic, which were originally published in special issues of *Narrative Inquiry*, along with four commentaries per article, and a final response from the author, addressing issues brought up in the commentaries.

Bal, M. (1985). *Narratology*. Toronto: University of Toronto Press.

A classic introduction to narratology. For a sense of how to approach life story written texts, for instance, this is an extremely helpful resource. At the same time, some of these insights can usefully be translated outside of written texts to other forms of narrative.

Bell, S. (2009). *DES Daughters: Embodied Knowledge and the Transformation of Women's Health Politics*. Philadelphia, PA: Temple University Press.

This book presents some long-term work with women affected by an anti-nausea drug taken by their mothers during pregnancy, which has effects of varying frequency and severity on their reproductive tracts. For narrative researchers, it brings together issues of narratives and activism, narratives in the health field, the significance of moving and still visual narratives and the way in which narrative structures may be inflected by social and personal histories.

Boonzaier, F. (2019). 'Researching Sex Work: Doing Decolonial, Intersectional Narrative Analysis'. In J. Fleetwood, L. Presser, S. Sandbert and T. Ugelvik (eds), *Emerald Handbook of Narrative Criminology*. Bingley: Emerald Press.

An extremely helpful account of bringing together concerns with narrative, intersectionality, decoloniality and social justice.

Bradbury, J. (2019). *Narrative Psychology and Vygotsky in Dialogue*. New York: Oxford University Press.

This book brings Vygotsky's work together with narrative research to consider the history and possible futures of South Africa and other countries living with the unequal legacies of colonialism and to posit lines of personal and political change. The author is also a co-founder of South Africa's Narrative Enquiry for Social Transformation network.

Brockmeier, J. (2015). *Beyond the Archive: Memory, Narrative and the Autobiographical Process*. New York: Oxford University Press.

A wide-ranging, multidisciplinary consideration of memory and its relation to narrative across cognition but also lived practices.

Bruner, J. (1990). *Acts of Meaning*. Cambridge, MA: Harvard University Press.

Bruner's emphasis on the significance of narrative for understanding human life has had a major influence on narrative research in psychology. Here, he poses personal and cultural narrative repertoires as psychological research objects against the computations, abstractions and models favoured by much cognitive psychology.

Bury, M. (1982). 'Chronic Illness as Biographical Disruption'. *Sociology of Health and Illness* 4: 167–82 (see also Bury, 2001).

Michael Bury's work on illness narratives was the first to suggest a powerful connection between health trajectory and biographical course. Later revised, it has had a continuing and powerful effect on the health and illness narrative field.

Caetano, A., and M. Nico (2022). *Biographical Research: Challenges and Creativity*. London: Routledge.

A fresh and comprehensive take on contemporary possibilities for biographical research.

Canham, H. K. (2023). *Riotous Deathscapes*. Chapel Hill, NC: Duke University Press.

A radical imaginative narrative meditation on rural Black African lives and theories and their social, political, environmental and global relations.

Carver, N. (2021). *Marriage, Gender and Refugee Migration*. London: Routledge.

An insightful approach to narratives told by Somali migrants and refugees living in the UK, in which narratives' imbrication in 'context' and complexity of 'form' are worked with in parallel.

Carolissen, R., and P. Kiguwa (2018). 'Narrative Explorations of the Micro-Politics of Students' Citizenship, Belonging and Alienation at South African Universities'. *South African Journal of Higher Education* 32 (3): 1–111.

This work brings together the ways of seeing differently, and seeing more, that are made possible by narrative explorations of students' lives within historically racialized and racist South African universities and broader sociopolitical formations.

Charon, R., S. DasGupta, N. Hermann, C. Irvine, E. Marcus et al. (2016). *The Principles and Practice of Narrative Medicine*. New York: Oxford University Press.

This edited collection includes chapters on teaching narrative, narrative ethics, intersubjectivity and queer health.

Culler, J. (2002). *The Pursuit of Signs*. Ithaca, NY: Cornell University Press.

First published in 1981, this book is an overarching and assured introduction to semiotics that, in its section on narrative, deconstructs the *fabula–syuzhet* division and manages to shoehorn Freudian case histories and Labovian event narratives into the same chapter.

Clandinin, J., V. Caine and S. Lessard (2018). *The Relational Ethics of Narrative Inquiry*. New York: Routledge.

A programme for narrative inquiry as a relational project: A must-read.

Davis, M., G. Bolding, G. Hart, L. Sherr and J. Elford (2004). 'Reflecting on the Experience of Interviewing Online: Perspectives from the Internet and HIV Study in London'. *AIDS Care* 16 (8): 944–52.

Contains examples of synchronous online interviews and discusses them in terms of the structures of address that shape online narrative practices.

Davis, M. (2011). '"You Have to Come into the World": Transition, Emotion and Being in Narratives of Life with the Internet'. *Somatechnics* 1 (2): 253–71.

This paper examines the narratives of the social impact of social media in connection with personal experience accounts of the advent of social media in the life course.

An important accompaniment to jeremiads against and apologias for new-media lives, the article demonstrates the complexities that narrative research can bring to bear within such arguments. Here, personal stories express not only the shaping effects of media on subjectivities but also the extent to which existing patterns of subjectivity override and co-opt such media.

Davis, M., and D. Lohm (2020). *Pandemics, Publics and Narrative*. New York: Oxford University Press.

An extremely timely book, pre-Covid-19, tracing overlapping public and private narratives of influenza as a guide to the stories of illness, vaccination, isolation and contagion likely to arise in all future pandemic contexts.

De Fina, A., and A. Georgakopoulou (2015). *Handbook of Narrative Analysis*. London: Wiley.

A helpfully broad collection focusing on the process within narrative research that may generate the most doubt and delay.

Elliott, J. (ed.) (2005). *Using Narrative in Social Research: Qualitative and Quantitative Approaches*. London: Sage.

This chapter gives a clear overview of some of the key issues, which are often a part of narrative research – including ethical issues. It uses concrete examples and indicates other useful sources. The book is an extremely useful text, one of the few to bring together qualitative and quantitative approaches to narrative work.

Esin (2017). 'Telling Stories in Pictures: Constituting Processual and Relational Narratives in Research with Young British Muslim Women in East London'. *Forum Qualitative Sozialforschung / Forum: Qualitative Social Research* 18 (1). Article 15, January. https://www.qualitative-research.net/index.php/fqs/article/view/2774/4063.

Esin's articulation of her processual narrative framework, drawing on the spatiality, dialogism and co-construction involved with 'visual autobiographical' research.

Esin, C., and A. Lounasmaa (2020). 'Narrative and Ethical (In)action: Creating Spaces of Resistance with Refugee-Storytellers in the Calais "Jungle" Camp'. *International Journal of Social Research Methodology* 23 (4): 391–403. https://www.tandfonline.com/doi/abs/10.1080/13645579.2020.1723202.

Esin, C., M. Fathi and C. Squire (2013). 'A Social Constructionist Account of Narrative Analysis'. In U. Fleck (ed.). *Sage Handbook of Narrative Analysis*. London: Sage.

An exposition of constructionist, positioning, dialogic and performative approaches to narrative work and their relations to each other. This paper works with the concept of narrative hesitancy to address the inevitably compromised positioning of researching about/with people.

Fine, M., and A. Harris (eds) (2001). *Critical psychology*. Issue 4. Special Issue: Under the Covers: Theorizing the Politics of Counter-Stories.

This special issue of the journal *Critical Psychology* contains some excellent articles on the topic of 'counter-stories', drawing on their prior history within Critical Race Theory. The introduction helps to establish a framework for this important area of research.

Fludernik, M. (2010). *Towards a 'Natural' Narratology*. New York: Routledge.

A much-quoted text that integrates the linguistics of natural language storytelling with literary approaches (see also Herman's (2018) work and for a useful critical perspective, Hutto and Myin (2017)).

Frank, A. (1995/2013). *The Wounded Storyteller: Body, Illness, and Ethics*, 2nd edn. Chicago: University of Chicago Press.

This classic account of health and illness narratives introduces the categories of chaos, restitution and quest: a frame for narrative analysis still frequently invoked today.

Freeman, M. (1993). *Rewriting the Self: History, Memory, Narrative*. New York: Routledge.

A classic book that influentially discussed the ways in which narratives work across chronological time, recasting the past from the present and vice versa. Freeman's later (2009a) book revisits these important temporal complications in personal narratives.

Genette, G. (1967–70/1983) *Narrative Discourse: An Essay in Method*. Ithaca, NY: Cornell University Press.

The most complex and thorough poststructuralist account specifically of narrative (though also see Barthes, 1977; Culler, 2002; Todorov, 1990), based on analysis of Proust's *Remembrance of Things Past*. The book's effort to be comprehensive makes it a specially useful resource in a narratological field, which still often focuses, frequently without explicit justification, on highly particular features.

Georgakopoulou, A. (2022). 'Small Stories Research: A Narrative Paradigm for the Analysis of Social Media'. In L. Sloan and A. Quan-Haase (eds) *The Sage Handbook of Social Media Research Methods*, pp. 266–81. London: Sage.

A useful starting point for engagement with Georgakopoulou's approach to the structural analysis of social media narrative practices.

Georgakopoulou, A. (2007). *Small Stories, Interaction and Identities. Studies in Narrative 8*. Amsterdam/Philadelphia: John Benjamins.

This book exemplifies the careful address to how narratives work within the micro-contexts of everyday lives, that characterizes the 'small stories' approach to narrative work (see also Bamberg, 2006).

Harrison, B. (2009). *Life Story Research: Benchmarks in Social Research*. London: Sage.

A major compendium of life story work within social sciences, compiled, edited and introduced by a sociologist who has pioneered narrative work with visual materials (see also Harrison, 2010, 2005, 2002).

Hatavara, M., M. Hyvärinen, M. Mäkelä and F. Mäyrä (2016). *Narrative Theory, Literature, and New Media: Narrative Minds and Virtual Worlds*. London: Routledge.

This edited collection is an important resource for cultural studies analysts focused on narrative production after digital media.

Herman, D. (2018). *Narratology beyond the Human*. Oxford: Oxford University Press.

An important expansion of narrative research to consider non-human narrators and narrative subjects.

Hydén, L. C. (2011). 'Narrative Collaboration and Scaffolding in Dementia'. *Journal of Aging Studies* 25: 339–47.

This paper exemplifies L. C. Hydén's research on narrative co-construction in situations where losses of brain function inhibit conventional storytelling. In so doing, it points out the significance of narrative even in situations of severe cognitive and linguistic difficulty, where stories might seem to be minimal, even absent.

Hydén, L. C. (2018a). *Entangled Narratives: Collaborative Storytelling and the Re-Imagining of Dementia*. New York: Oxford University Press.

This book is about the possibilities of people living with dementia telling stories and taking part in conversational storytelling. The book discusses how to collect and analyse narrative material from people living with a communicative disability like dementia. The book also analyses how bodily resources are used for storytelling.

Hydén, M. (2010). 'Listening to Children's Experiences of Being Participant Witnesses to Domestic Violence'. In H. Forsberg and T. Kröger (eds) *Social Work and Child Welfare Politics: Through Nordic Lenses*, pp. 129–46. Bristol: Policy Press.

In this chapter, M. Hydén explores with us the contribution narrative work can make to understanding social research questions that are often either ignored or difficult to approach using conventional quantitative or qualitative methods. For a broader account of 'sensitive topics' research, see M. Hydén (2014).

Hyvarinen, M., L. C. Hydén, M. Saarenheimo and M. Tamboukou (2010). *Beyond Narrative Coherence*. Amsterdam: John Benjamins.

A landmark collection that brings together a diverse body of research on 'incoherence' in narratives, in the process articulating a strong criticism of assumptions about the essential, viable or even necessarily positive character of narrative coherence.

Josselson, R., and A. Lieblich (1993). *The Narrative Study of Lives*. Thousand Oaks, CA: Sage.

The first in a series under this title, dealing broadly with how to analyse personal stories in ways that deepen understanding and that have therapeutic and/or social significance.

Kleinman, A. (1988). *The Illness Narratives*. New York: Basic Books.

Kleinman's classic account of the value of listening to patients and understanding illness and suffering alongside disease and pathology is widely influential among medical and paramedical professionals.

Labov, W., and J. Waletsky (1967). 'Narrative Analysis: Oral Versions of Personal Experience'. In J. Helms (ed.) *Essays in the Verbal and Visual Arts*. Seattle, WA: University of Washington.

For narrative researchers, this chapter is the first systematic attempt to explain story structure in a socially embedded way. Labov's (1997) updating is also important to read. However, really to understand his work in context, *Language in the Inner City*, his account of his wide-ranging research project on Black English Vernacular (1972) is indispensable.

Luttrell, W. (2020). *Children Framing Childhoods*. Bristol: Policy Press. Also https://www.childrenframingchildhoods.com/.

This book and website follow an unusually dedicated longitudinal narrative research project, which has grown up alongside the children with whom it works.

Mitchell, C., N. de Lange and R. Molestane (2017). *Participatory Visual Methodologies: Social Change, Community and Policy*. London: Sage.

Claudia Mitchell, with her co-researchers, has carried out significant work with communities using various visual methodologies, particularly in the field of education and HIV/AIDS in Southern Africa, and as such has addressed not only the kinds of narrative that they may produce but how they may be practical tools for participatory inquiry with social change and democratic possibilities. At the same time, she also pays considerable attention to how we should conceptualize and problematize their use. (See also her 2012 volume *Doing Visual Research*. London: Sage.)

Meretoja, H. (2018). *The Ethics of Storytelling: Narrative Hermeneutics, History, and the Possible*. New York: Oxford University Press.

This book develops a new theoretical-analytic framework for exploring the ethical potential of narratives.

Mishler, E. (1986/1995). *Research Interviewing: Context and Narrative*. Cambridge, MA: Harvard University Press.

A classic text, still much used. The chapters detailing Mishler's adaptation of Labovian frameworks and his understanding of the contexts and multiple truths of narratives are still particularly useful.

Namiba, A. et al. (2023). *Our Stories Told by Us*. London: Zouk Press.

An exemplary piece of community-based, collective narrative research.

Page, R. (2018). *Narratives Online: Shared Stories in Social Media*. Cambridge: Cambridge University Press.

An important methods primer for analysts researching social media narratives.

Phoenix, A., J. Brannen and C. Squire (2021). *Researching Family Narratives*. London: Sage.

This book documents a multi-centre collaborative research initiative, built up from five separate projects: Narratives of everyday lives and linked approaches (NOVELLA), working across the UK and India. It exemplifies the entanglement of ethics, politics and relationality and the attention to variable narrative media and modalities, and as the project title suggests, embeds narrative theory within method.

Plummer, K. (2019). *Narrative Power*. London: Sage.

This book explores what Plummer identifies as the key dimension of narrative power, focusing on how narratives of suffering can change through transformative narrative actions.

Polletta, F. (2006). *It Was like a Fever: Storytelling in Protest and Politics*. Chicago: University of Chicago Press.

This highly readable book analyses how stories are used in a number of different contexts (courtrooms, newsrooms, public forums, the US Congress) and demonstrates the power of storytelling in strategic political mobilization.

Ricoeur, P. (1984). *Time and Narrative*. Chicago: University of Chicago Press.

An important reference for all interested in the relationships of stories to temporality and for phenomenological approaches to narrative work. For a condensed and readable version of his account of narrative research as hermeneutics, see also Ricoeur (1991).

Riessman, C. (2008). *Narrative Methods for the Human Sciences*. New York: Sage.

A comprehensive account of contemporary narrative work by one of the foremost researchers in the field. An invaluable overview for those starting out.

Rogers, R. (2019). *Doing Digital Methods*. London: Sage

As we have suggested in this volume, both textual and visual narratives may increasingly be found on digital and social media platforms. It is important that narrative researchers understand the particular issues which arise in relation to the production and then the use and analysis of this material. This text covers the use of digital devices, search engines and social media platforms with case studies. Many general texts now include chapters on digital methods and materials also.

Ryan, M. (2022). *A New Anatomy of Storyworlds*. Ohio: University Press.

An ambitious interdisciplinary exploration that ties narrative to all aspects of the human world.

Schachtner, C. (2020). *The Narrative Subject: Storytelling in the Age of the Internet*. London: Palgrave.

This book provides a comprehensive primer for the narrative researcher of digital and social media, offering theoretical framing of the field and a practical guide inquiry.

Selbin, E. (2010). *Revolution, Rebellion, Resistance: The Power of Story*. London: Zed Books.

This book looks at how past injustices are reworked through stories and how they are used in the struggle to create a better world.

Squire, C. (2021). *Stories Changing Lives*. New York: Oxford University Press.

One of a number of contemporary attempts (e.g. Polletta, 2006) to map how narratives may produce the kinds of positive social changes with which they are, often without much evidence, associated.

Stanley, L. (1995). *The Auto/biographical I*. Manchester: Manchester University Press.

A powerfully influential feminist framing of autobiographical and biographical genres, relating them consistently to the material world and histories, and deploying the slashed division within auto/biography to alert us to the ways in which the two genres are connected within feminist work.

Tamboukou, M. (2017). *Women Workers' Education, Life Narratives and Politics*. London: Palgrave.

A persuasive account of how the autobiographical writing of feminist working-class women activists has shaped twentieth-century western cultural and political formations.

Wright Mills, C. (1959). *The Sociological Imagination*. London: Oxford University Press.

A programmatic statement on the social sciences, again from a humanist perspective, calling for attention to the personal and historical as well as the social dimensions of sociological research. Still much cited and drawn on by contemporary narrative researchers.

REFERENCES

Abdi, M. (2023). *Somali Students' School Experiences*. London: Palgrave.
Adichie, C. (2009). 'The Danger of a Single Story'. TEDGlobal, July. https://www.ted.com/talks/chimamanda_ngozi_adichie_the_danger_of_a_single_story?language=en. Accessed 6 October 2023.
Africa et al. (Calais Writers) (2017). *Voices from the Jungle*. London: Pluto.
Ahmed, S. (2021). *Complaint!* Durham, NC: Duke University Press.
Alam, S. (2008). 'Majority World: Challenging the West's Rhetoric of Democracy'. *Amerasia Journal* 34 (1): 87–98.
Alwan, N. A. (2021). 'The Road to Addressing Long Covid'. *Science*, 30 July, 373 (6554): 491–3.
Amaral, A., A.-K. Jung, L.-M. Braun and B. Blanco (2022). 'Narratives of Anti-Vaccination Movements in the German and Brazilian Twittersphere: A Grounded Theory Approach'. *Media and Communication* 10 (2): 144–56.
Anderson, E. (2010). 'Telling Stories: Unreliable Discourse, Fight Club, and the Cinematic Narrator'. *Journal of Narrative Theory* 40 (1): 80–107.
Andrews, M. (1991/2008). *Lifetimes of Commitment: Aging, Politics, Psychology*. Cambridge: Cambridge University Press.
Andrews, M. (2002). 'Generational Consciousness, Dialogue, and Political Engagement'. In J. Edmunds and B. Turner (eds). *Generational Consciousness, Narrative, and Politics*, pp. 75–88. Lanham, MD: Rowman and Littlefield.
Andrews, M. (2004). 'Counter-Narratives and the Power to Oppose'. In M. Bamberg and M. Andrews (eds). *Considering Counter-Narratives: Narrating, Resisting, Making Sense*, pp. 1–6. Amsterdam: John Benjamins.
Andrews, M. (2007). *Shaping History*. Cambridge: Cambridge University Press.
Andrews, M. (2014). *Narrative Imagination and Everyday Life*. New York: Oxford University Press.

Andrews, M. (2017a). 'Political Narratives and Abraham Obama'. *Oxford Research Encyclopedia of Politics*. Oxford: Oxford University Press.

Andrews, M. (2017b) 'Popular Representation of East Germany: Whose History Is It?'. In H. Meretoja and C. Davis (eds). *Storytelling and Ethics: Culture, Visual Arts and the Power of Narrative*, pp. 174–89. New York: Taylor and Francis.

Andrews, M. (2021). 'Quality Indicators in Narrative Research'. *Qualitative Research in Psychology* 18 (3): 353–68.

Andrews, M. and M. Freeman (forthcoming). 'Certainty and Uncertainty in Pandemic Storytelling: Tales from the US, the UK, and Beyond'. In Jan Alber, Deborah de Muijnck and Jessica Jempertz (eds). *Pandemic Storytelling*. Leiden, NL: Brill.

Andrews, M., C. Squire and M. Tamboukou (2013). *Doing Narrative Research*, 2nd edn. London: Sage.

Annabell, T. (2022). '"Sharing for the Memories": Contemporary Conceptualizations of Memories by Young Women'. *Memory Studies* 15 (6): 1544–56.

Anzaldúa, G. (1987). *Borderlands/La Frontera: The New Mestiza*. San Francisco: Aunt Lute Books.

Aristotle (350 BC). *The Ethics of Aristotle*. The Project Gutenberg eBook of The Nicomachean Ethics of Aristotle, by Aristotle. https://www.gutenberg.org/files/8438/8438-h/8438-h.htm. Accessed 4 July 2024.

Atkinson, P. (2009). 'Illness Narratives Revisited: The Failure of Narrative Reductionism'. *Sociological Research Online* 14 (5): 16. https://doi.org/10.5153/sro.2030.

Baker, M. (2006). *Translation and Conflict: A Narrative Account*. London: Routledge.

Bakhtin, M. (1982). *The Dialogic Imagination*. Austin: Texas University Press.

Bal, M. (2020). 'Telling Objects'. In D. Preziosi and C. Farago (eds). *Grasping the World*, pp. 84–102. London: Routledge

Bal, M. (1985). *Narratology*. Toronto: University of Toronto Press.

Bamberg, M. (2004). 'Considering Counter-Narratives'. In M. Bamberg and M. Andrews (eds). *Considering Counter-Narratives: Narrating, Resisting, Making Sense*, pp. 351–71. Amsterdam: John Benjamins.

Bamberg, M. (2006). 'Stories: Big or Small: Why Do We Care?' *Narrative Inquiry* 16 (1): 139–47. DOI:https://doi.org/10.1075/ni.16.1.18bam.

Bamberg, M., and M. Andrews (2004). *Considering Counter-Narratives: Narrating, Resisting, Making Sense*. Amsterdam: John Benjamins.

Bamberg, M., and Z. Wipff (2020). 'Counter-Narratives of Crime and Punishment'. In M. Althoff, B. Martina, Bernd Dollinger and H. Holger

Schmidt (eds). *Conflicting Narratives of Crime and Punishment*, pp. 23–41. Switzerland: Palgrave Macmillan.

Barret, D., L. Ortmann and S. Larson (eds) (2022). *Narrative Ethics in Public Health: The Value of Stories*. New York: Springer.

Barthes, R. (1977). *The Pleasures of the Text*. New York: Hill and Wang.

Barthes, R. (1981). *Camera Lucida*. New York: Noonday Press.

Bartholomeusz, S. (2018). 'Big Data Backlash: Consumers Wise Up to Facebook, Twitter'. *Sydney Morning Herald Online*. https://www.smh.com.au/business/consumer-affairs/big-data-backlash-consumers-wise-up-to-facebook-twitter-20180730-p4zuea.html. Accessed 18 September 2019.

Baele, S., L. Brace and T. G. Coan (2019). 'From "Incel" to "Saint": Analyzing the Violent Worldview behind the 2018 Toronto Attack'. *Terrorism and Political Violence* 33 (8): 1667–91. https://doi.org/10.1080/09546553.2019.1638256.

Bell, S. (2009). *DES Daughters: Embodied Knowledge and the Transformation of Women's Health Politics*. Philadelphia, PA: Temple University Press.

Bengtsson, T., and D. Andersen (2020). 'Narrative Analysis – Thematic, Structural, Performative'. In M. Jarvinen and N. Mik-Meyer (eds). *Qualitative Analysis*, pp. 265–82. London: Sage.

Berger, J., and J. Mohr (1982). *Another Way of Telling*. London: Vantage.

Bernstein, M. (1994). *Foregone Conclusions: Against Apocalyptic History*. Berkeley: California University Press.

Beverley, J. (2004). *Testimonio: On the Politics of Truth*. Minneapolis: University of Minnesota Press.

Bhabha, H. (2010). 'The Right to Narrate'. *Harvard Design Magazine* 38. https://www.harvarddesignmagazine.org/articles/the-right-to-narrate/. Accessed 3 October 2023.

Biko, S. (2002). *I Write What I Like*. Chicago: IL: University of Chicago Press.

Bjorninen, S., M. Hatavara, M. Makela (2020). 'Narrative as Social Action: A Narratological Approach to Story, Discourse and Positioning in Political Storytelling'. *International Journal of Social Research Methodology* 23 (4): 437–49.

Boden, D., and D. Zimmerman (1993). *Talk and Social Structure*. Cambridge: Polity.

Boje, D. (2001). *Narrative Methods for Organisational and Communication Research*. Thousand Oaks, CA: Sage.

Boonzaier, F. (2019). 'Researching Sex Work: Doing Decolonial, Intersectional Narrative Analysis'. In J. Fleetwood, L. Presser, S. Sandbert and T. Ugelvik (eds). *Emerald Handbook of Narrative Criminology*, pp. 467–91. Bingley: Emerald Press.

Boonzaier, F., I. Katsere, S. Mulubale, S. Peters, A. Prates and C. Squire (2024). 'Narrating Lives with HIV and COVID-19; Narratives as COVID-19 Theory'. In L. Moran and Z. Dooley (eds). *Biographical Perspectives on Lives Lived During Covid-19*, 123–45. New York: Springer.

Bourdieu, P. (1990). *Photography: A Middle-Brow Art*. Cambridge: Polity.

Bradbury, J. (2019). *Narrative Psychology and Vygotsky in Dialogue*. New York: Oxford University Press.

Brännlund, E., T. Kovacic and A. Lounasmaa (2013). 'Narratives in/of Translations: A Trialogue on Translating Narratives Cross-Culturally'. *Narrative Works* 3 (2): 72–91.

Braun, V., and V. Clarke (2021). *Thematic Analysis: A Practical Guide*. London: Sage.

Brockmeier, J. (2015). *Beyond the Archive: Memory, Narrative and the Autobiographical Process*. New York: Oxford University Press.

Bruner, J. (1990). *Acts of Meaning*. Cambridge, MA: Harvard University Press.

Bruner, J. (2002). *Making Stories: Law, Literature, Life*. New York: Farrar, Straus and Giroux.

Burgon, J., and J. Green (2018). *You Tube: Online Video and Participatory Culture*, London: Wiley.

Bury, M. (1982). 'Chronic Illness as Biographical Disruption'. *Sociology of Health and Illness* 4: 167–82.

Bury, M. (2001). 'Illness Narratives: Fact or Fiction'. *Sociology of Health and Illness* 23: 263–85.

Butina, M. (2015). 'A Narrative Approach to Qualitative Inquiry'. *Clinical Laboratory Science* 28 (3): 190–6.

Butler, J. (2005). *Giving an Account of Oneself*. Bronx, NY: Fordham University Press.

Caetano, A., and M. Nico (2022). *Biographical Research: Challenges and Creativity*. London: Routledge.

Canham, H. K. (2023). *Riotous Deathscapes*. Chapel Hill, NC: Duke University Press.

Cardinal, T., S. Murphy and J. Huber (2019). 'Movements toward Living Relationally Ethical Assessment Making: Bringing Indigenous Ways of Being, Knowing, and Doing Alongside Narrative Inquiry as Pedagogy'. *Revista Interuniversitaria de Formación del Profesorado* 33 (3): 121–40. Universidad de Zarag. https://www.redalyc.org/journal/274/2746 6132007/27466132007.pdf. Accessed 28 June 2024.

Carolissen, R., and P. Kiguwa (2018). 'Narrative Explorations of the Micro-Politics of Students' Citizenship, Belonging and Alienation at South African Universities'. *South African Journal of Higher Education* 32 (3): 1–111.

Carver, N. (2021). *Marriage, Gender and Refugee Migration: Spousal Relationships among Somali Muslims in the UK*. New Brunswick, NJ: Rutgers University Press.

Cavieres-Fernandez, E. (2017). 'Teacher Counter Stories to a Citizenship Education Mega Policy Narrative. Preparing for Citizenship in Chile'. *Journal of Curriculum Studies* 49 (4): 414–36.

Charon, R. (2006). *Narrative Medicine: Honoring the Stories of Illness*. Oxford: Oxford University Press.

Chungara, D. (1978). *Let Me Speak!* New York: Monthly Review Press.

Clandinin, D., and M. Connelly (2004). *Narrative Inquiry: Experience and Story in Qualitative Research*. San Francisco: Jossey-Bass.

Clandinin, D., V. Caine and S. Lessard (2018). *The Relational Ethics of Narrative Inquiry*. New York: Routledge.

Clandinin, D., and J. Rosiek (2019). 'Mapping a Landscape of Narrative Inquiry: Borderland Spaces and Tension'. In D. Clandinin (ed.). *Journeys in Narrative Inquiry*, pp. 228–64. New York: Routledge.

Clark, A., I. Ahmed, S. Metzger, E. Walker and R. Wylie (2022). 'Moving from Co-Design to Co-Research: Engaging Youth Participation in Guided Qualitative Inquiry'. *International Journal of Qualitative Methods* 21. https://doi.org/10.1177/16094069221084793.

Clark, E., and E. Mishler (1992). "Attending to Patients' Stories: Reframing the Clinical Task'. *Sociology of Health and Illness* 14 (3): 344–70.

Connell, R. W., M. Davis and G. Dowsett (1993). 'A Bastard of a Life: Homosexual Desire and Practice among Men in Working-Class Milieux'. *Australian and New Zealand Journal of Sociology* 29 (1): 211–35.

Crow, G. (2022). '"Amusing and Fun", "Arresting" or the "Wrong Pictures"? Methodological Lessons from Using Photo Elicitation in a Study of Academic Retirement'. *Sociological Research Online* 29 (1): 3–22. https://doi.org/10.1177/13607804221133117.

Culler, J. (2002). *The Pursuit of Signs*. Ithaca, NY: Cornell University Press.

Dadzie, S., B. Bryan and S. Scafe (2018) *Heart of the Race*. London: Verso.

Davies, B., and R. Harre (1990). 'Positioning: The Discursive Construction of Selves'. *Journal for the Theory of Social Behaviour* 20: 43–63.

Davis, M. (2011). '"You Have to Come into the World": Transition, Emotion and Being in Narratives of Life with the Internet. *Somatechnics* 1(2): 253–71.

Davis, M. (2017). '"Is It Going to Be Real?" Narrative and Media on a Pandemic, Symposium on Analyzing Narratives across Media'. *Forum Qualitative Sozialforschung / Forum: Qualitative Social Research* 18

(4). Article 18. https://www.qualitative-research.net/index.php/fqs/article/view/2768.
Davis, M., and P. Flowers (2011). 'Love and HIV Serodiscordance in Gay Men's Accounts of Life with Their Regular Partners'. *Culture, Health and Sexuality* 13 (7): 737–49.
Davis, M., and P. Flowers (2014). 'HIV/STI Prevention Technologies and Strategic (In)visibilities'. In M. Davis and L. Manderson (eds). *Disclosure in Health and Illness*, pp. 72–88. London: Routledge.
Davis, M., and D. Lohm (2020). *Pandemics, Publics and Narrative*. New York: Oxford University Press.
De Fina, A. (2016). 'Storytelling and Audience Reactions in Social Media', *Language in Society* 45: 473–98.
De Fina, A., and A. Georgakopoulou (2015). *Handbook of Narrative Analysis*. London: Wiley.
De Fina, A., and B. Johnstone (2015). 'Discourse Analysis and Narrative'. In D. Tannen, H. Hamilton and D. Schiffrin (eds). *Handbook of Discourse Analysis 2*, pp. 152–67. New York: Wiley.
Del Tufo, A., M. Fine, L. Cahill, C. Okaofor and D. Cook (2021). 'The Power of Bearing Wit(h)ness: Intergenerational Storytelling about Racial Violence, Healing and Resistance'. In C. Squire (ed.). *Stories Changing Lives*. New York: Oxford University Press.
Derrida, J. (1979). 'Living On: Border-Lines'. In H. Bloom, P. De Man, H. Derrida, G. Hartman and J. H. Miller (eds). *Deconstruction and Criticism*, pp. 102–3. NewYork: Seabury Press.
Dewey, J. (1892). *Psychology*. United States: American Book Company.
Eagle Heart, S. (n.d.). 'Climate and Indigenous Storytelling: An Interview with Sarah Eagle Heart'. Good Energy Stories. https://www.goodenergystories.com/playbook/climate-and-indigenous-storytelling-an-interview-with-sarah-eagle-heart. Accessed 22 May 2023.
Eakin, P. (2020). *Writing Life Writing*. New York: Routledge.
Elliott, J. (2005). *Using Narrative in Social Research: Qualitative and Quantitative Approaches*. London: Sage.
Elliott, H., C. Squire and R. O'Connell (2017). 'Narratives of Normativity and Permissible Transgression: Mothers' Blogs about Mothering, Family and Food in Resource-Constrained Times'. *Forum Qualitative Sozialforschung / Forum: Qualitative Social Research* 18 (1). https://doi.org/10.17169/fqs-18.1.2775.
Esin (2017). 'Telling Stories in Pictures: Constituting Processual and Relational Narratives in Research with Young British Muslim Women in East London'. *Forum Qualitative Sozialforschung / Forum: Qualitative Social Research* 18 (1). Article 15, January.

https://www.qualitative-research.net/index.php/fqs/article/view/2774. Accessed 3 October 2023.

Esin, C., M. Fathi and C. Squire (2013). 'A Social Constructionist Account of Narrative Analysis'. In U. Flick (ed.). *Sage Handbook of Narrative Analysis*, pp. 203–16. London: Sage.

Esin, C., and L. Lounasmaa (2020). 'Narrative and Ethical (In)action: Creating Spaces of Resistance with Refugee-Storytellers in the Calais "Jungle" Camp'. *International Journal of Social Research Methodology* 23 (4): 391–403.

Esin, C., and C. Squire (2013). 'Visual Autobiographies in East London: Narratives of Still Images, Interpersonal Exchanges, and Intrapersonal Dialogues'. *Forum Qualitative Sozialforschung / Forum: Qualitative Social Research* 14 (2). http://www.qualitative-research.net/index.php/fqs/article/view/1971. Accessed 31 December 2013.

Fathi, M. (2023). '"City as Home": Conducting Walking Interviews as Biographical Method with Migrant Men in Cork'. *Irish Journal of Sociology* 31 (1): 82–100.

Fernandes, S. (2017). 'Stories and Statecraft: Afghan Women's Narratives and the Construction of Western Freedoms'. *Signs: Journal of Women in Culture and Society* 42 (3): 643–67.

Fine, M., and M. Torre (2021). *Essentials of Critical Participatory Action Research*. Washington, DC: American Psychological Association.

Fleetwood, J., L. Presser, S. Sandberg and T. Ugelvik (2019). *The Emerald Handbook of Narrative Criminology*. Leeds: Emerald Publishing.

Flowers, P., and M. Davis (2013). 'Understanding the Biopsychosocial Aspects of HIV Disclosure amongst HIV Positive Gay Men in Scotland'. *Journal of Health Psychology* 18 (5): 711–24.

Fludernik, M. (2010). *Towards a 'Natural' Narratology*. New York: Routledge.

Foucault, M. (1980). *Power/Knowledge: Selected Interviews and Other Writings*. C. Gordon (ed.). New York: Pantheon.

Foucault, M. (1994). *The Order of Things*. New York: Random House.

Foucault, M. (1998). *The History of Sexuality 1 – the Will to Knowledge*. Harmondsworth: Penguin.

Frank, A. (1995/2013). *The Wounded Storyteller: Body, Illness, and Ethics*, 2nd edn. Chicago, IL: University of Chicago Press.

Frank, A. (2006). 'Health Stories as Connectors and Subjectifiers'. *Health* 10 (4): 421–40.

Freeman, M. (1993). *Rewriting the Self: History, Memory, Narrative*. New York: Routledge.

Freeman, M. (2003). 'Identity and Difference in Narrative Inquiry, Psychoanalytic Narratives: Writing the Self into Contemporary Cultural Phenomena'. *Narrative Inquiry* 13 (2): 331–46.
Freeman, M. (2009). *Hindsight: The Promises and Perils of Looking Backward*. New York: Oxford University Press.
Freeman, M. (2012). 'The Narrative Unconscious'. *Contemporary Psychoanalysis* 48 (3): 344–66.
Freeman, M. (2015). 'Narrative as a Mode of Understanding'. In A. De Fina and A. Georgakopoulou (eds). *Handbook of Narrative Analysis*, pp. 21–37. London: Wiley.
Gates, H. (1995). 'Thirteen Ways of Looking at a Black Man'. *New Yorker*, 16 October: 57. https://www.newyorker.com/magazine/1995/10/23/thirteen-ways-of-looking-at-a-black-man. Accessed 13 August 2024.
Gee, J. (1991). 'A Linguistic Approach to Narrative'. *Journal of Narrative and Life History* 1 (1): 15–39.
Genette, G. (1967–70/1983). *Narrative Discourse: An Essay in Method*. Ithaca, NY: Cornell University Press.
Georgakopoulou, A. (2007). *Small Stories, Interaction and Identities. Studies in Narrative 8*. Amsterdam/Philadelphia: John Benjamins.
Georgakopoulou, A. (2022). 'Small Stories Research: A Narrative Paradigm for the Analysis of Social Media. In L. Sloan and A. Quan-Haase (eds). *The Sage Handbook of Social Media Research Methods*, pp. 266–81. London: Sage.
Gergen, K. (1991). *The Saturated Self*. New York: Basic Books.
Giaxoglu, K. (2018). '#JeSuisCharlie? Hashtags as Narrative Resources in Contexts of Ecstatic Sharing'. *Discourse, Context & Media* 22: 13–20.
Gobodo-Madikizela, P. (2003). *A Human Being Died That Night*. Cape Town: David Phillip.
Goodson, I., A. Antikainen, P. Sikes and M. Andrews (eds) (2017). *The Routledge International Handbook on Narrative and Life History*. London: Routledge.
Goodwin, C. (2003). 'The Body in Action'. In J. Coupland and R. Gwyn (eds). *Discourse, the Body and Identity*, pp. 19–42. Gordonsville: Palgrave Macmillan.
Goodwin, D., N. Mays and C. Pope (2020). 'Ethical Issues in Qualitative Research'. In C. Pope and N. Mays (eds). *Qualitative Research in Health Care*, 4th edn, pp. 27–41. New Jersey: John Wiley.
Graffy, P., S. McKinnon, G. Lee and P. Remington (2019). 'Life Outside: A Narrative Ethnographic Inquiry into the Determinants of Homelessness'. *Journal for Poverty* 23 (3): 202–28.
Grattan, S. (2019). 'ACT-UP and the Queer Commons'. *Minnesota Review* 93: 126–32. DOI: 10.1215/00265667-7737353.

Gready, P. (2008). 'The Public Life of Narratives: Ethics, Politics, Methods'. In M. Andrews, C. Squire and M. Tamboukou (eds). *Doing Narrative Research*, pp. 137–50. London: Sage.

Greenhalgh, T. (2006). *What Seems to Be the Trouble? Stories in Illness and Healthcare*. Oxford: Radcliffe Publishing.

Greenhalgh, T., and B. Hurwitz (1999). 'Narrative Based Medicine: Why Study Narrative?'. *British Medical Journal* 318: 48.

Greenspan, H. (1998). *On Listening to Holocaust Survivors: Recounting and Life History*. London: Praeger.

Gubrium, J., and J. Holstein (2008). *Analyzing Narrative Reality*. London: Sage.

Hage, G. (2015). *Alter-Politics*. Melbourne: Melbourne University Press.

Hall, C. (2015). 'Narrative in Social Work'. In *International Encyclopaedia of the Social and Behavioural Sciences*, pp. 204–10. Amsterdam: Elsevier.

Hammack, P., B. Grecco, B. Wilson and I. Meyer (2022). '"White, Tall, Top, Masculine, Muscular": Narratives of Intracommunity Stigma in Young Sexual Minority Men's Experience on Mobile Apps. *Archives of Sexual Behaviour* 51: 2413–28.

Harris, A., S. Carney and M. Fine (2001). 'Counter Work: Introduction to Under the Covers: Theorising the Politics of Counter Stories'. *International Journal of Critical Psychology* 4 (2): 6–18.

Harrison, B. (2002). 'Photographic Visions and Narrative Inquiry'. *Narrative Inquiry* 12: 87–111.

Harrison, B. (2005). 'Snap Happy: Toward a Sociology of "Everyday" Photography. In C. Pole (ed.). *Seeing Is Believing: Visual Methods in Social Research*, pp. 23–38. London: Elsevier.

Harrison, B. (2009). *Life Story Research: Benchmarks in Social Research*. London: Sage.

Harrison, B. (2010). 'Amateur Photography as Life Writing'. Unpublished paper presented to the Conference of the International Autobiography Association, University of Sussex.

Harper, D (2002). 'Talking about Pictures: A Case for Photo Elicitation', *Visual Studies* 27 (1): 13–26 Published online 2010, original publication from 2002 https://www.tandfonline.com/doi/abs/10.1080/14725860220137345. Accessed 13 September 2024.

Hatavara, M., M. Hyvärinen, M. Mäkelä and F. Mäyrä (2016). *Narrative Theory, Literature, and New Media: Narrative Minds and Virtual Worlds*. London: Routledge.

Hawkins, A. (1998). *Reconstructing Illness: Studies in Pathography*. West Lafayette: Purdue University Press.

Hennessy, M., R. Dennehy, J. Doherty and K. O'Donoghue (2022). 'Outsourcing Transcription: Extending Ethical Considerations in Qualitative Research'. *Qualitative Health Research* 32 (7): 1197–204.

Henriques, J., W. Hollway, C. Urwin, C. Venn and V. Walkerdine (1984/1998). *Changing the Subject*. London: Routledge/Methuen.

Herman, D. (2013). 'Approaches to Narrative Worldmaking'. In M. Andrews, C. Squire and M. Tamboukou (eds). *Doing Narrative Research*, 2nd edn, pp. 176–96. London: Sage.

Herman, D. (2018). *Narratology beyond the Human*. Oxford: Oxford University Press.

Himmelfarb, G. (1984). 'The Idea of Poverty'. *History Today* 34 (4). http://www.historytoday.com/gertrude-himmelfarb/idea-poverty. Accessed 14 May 2014.

Hollway, W., and T. Jefferson (2012). *Doing Qualitative Research Differently: Free Association, Narrative and the Interview Method*, 2nd edn. London: Sage.

Holstein, J., and J. Gubrium (eds) (2008). *Handbook of Constructionist Research*. New York: Guilford Press.

hooks, b. (1999). *Remembered Rapture. The Writer at Work*. New York: Henry Holt.

Horton, R. (2019). 'Offline: The False Narrative of "tremendous progress"'. *The Lancet* 394 (10204): 1129. https://www.thelancet.com/journals/lancet/article/PIIS0140-6736(19)32208-1/fulltext. Accessed 6 October 2023.

Hull, G., B. Scott and B. Smith (2015). *But Some of Us Are Brave*. London: Feminist Press.

Hutto, D., and E. Myin (2008/2012). *Folk Psychological Narratives*. Cambridge, MA: MIT Press.

Hutto, D., and E. Myin (2017). *Evolving Enactivism*. Cambridge, MA: MIT Press.

Hydén, L. C. (2011). 'Narrative Collaboration and Scaffolding in Dementia'. *Journal of Aging Studies* 25: 339–47.

Hydén, L. C. (2013). 'Bodies, Embodiment and Stories'. In M. Andrews, C. Squire and M. Tamboukou (eds). *Doing Narrative Research*, pp. 126–41. London: Sage.

Hydén, L. C. (2018a). *Entangled Narratives, Collaborative Storytelling and the Re-Imagining of Dementia*. New York: Oxford University Press.

Hydén, L. C. (2018b). 'Stories, IIllness and Narrative Norms'. In G. Lucius-Hoene, T. Meyer and C. Holmberg (eds). *Illness Narratives in Practice*, pp. 40–51. New York: Oxford University Press.

Hydén, L. C., and E. Antelius (2011). 'Communicative Disability and Stories: Towards an Embodied Conception of Narratives'. *Health* 15: 594–609.

Hydén, M. (1995). *Kvinnomisshandel inom äktenskapet. Mellan det omöjliga och det möjliga*. Stockholm: Liber.

Hydén, M. (2010). 'Listening to Children's Experiences of Being Participant Witnesses to Domestic Violence'. In H. Forsberg and T. Kröger (eds). *Social Work and Child Welfare Politics: Through Nordic Lenses*, pp. 129–46. Bristol: Policy Press.

Hydén, M. (2013). 'Researching Sensitive Topics'. In M. Andrews, C. Squire and M. Tamboukou (eds). *Doing Narrative Research*, pp. 121–36. London: Sage.

Hydén, M. (2014). 'The Teller Focused Interview: Interviewing as Relational Practice'. *Qualitative Social Work*, 13 (6): 795–812. doi: 10.1177/1473325013506247.

Hydén, M. (2015). What Social Networks Do in the Aftermath of Domestic Violence. *British Journal of Criminology* 55 (6): 1040–57.

Hydén, M., D. Gadd and T. Grund (2020). 'Role of Narrative and Social Networks in Thwarting Violence and Sexual Abuse in Young People's Lives'. *British Journal of Social Work* 50: 2172–90.

Hyvarinen, M. (2021). 'Toward a Theory of Counter-Narratives: Narrative Contestation, Cultural Canonicity, and Tellability'. In K. Lueg and M. Lundholdt (eds). *Routledge Handbook of Counter-Narratives*, London: Routledge,17–29.

Hyvarinen, M., L. C. Hydén, M. Saarenheimo and M. Tamboukou (2010). *Beyond Narrative Coherence*. Amsterdam: John Benjamins.

Jaworska, S. (2018). '"Bad" Mums Tell the "Untellable": Narrative Practices and Agency in Online Stories about Postnatal Depression on Mumsnet', *Discourse, Context & Media* 25: 25–33.

Jolly, M. (2019). *Sisterhood and After: An Oral History of the UK Women's Liberation Movement, 1968-Present*. Oxford: Oxford University Press.

Josselson, R., and P. Hammack (2021). *Narrative Analysis*. Washington, DC: American Psychological Association.

Josselson, R., and A. Lieblich (1993). *The Narrative Study of Lives*. Thousand Oaks, CA: Sage.

Kavelina, D. (2020). *Letter to a Turtle Dove*. Short film. https://www.e-flux.com/film/339843/letter-to-a-turtledove/. Accessed 13 August 2024.

Kofoed, J., and D. Staunæs (2015). 'Hesitancy as Ethics'. *Reconceptualizing Educational Research Methodology* 6 (2): 24–39.

Kearns, C., and N. Kearns (2020). 'The Role of Comics in Public Health Communication during the COVID-19 Pandemic'. *Journal of Visual Communication in Medicine* 43: 139–49.

Kendon, A. (1990). *Conducting Interaction: Patterns of Behavior in Focused Encounters*. New York: Cambridge University Press.

Kennedy, H. (2003). 'Technobiography: Researching Lives Online and Off'. *Biography* 26 (1): 120–30.

Kessi, S. (2021). 'Cultural Identities and Narratives that "Race": Representations and Resistance in the Context of a South African University'. In C. Squire (ed.). *Stories Changing Lives*, pp. 164–84. New York: Oxford University Press.

Kessler, G., S. Rizzo and M. Kelley (2021). 'Trump's False or Misleading Claims Total 30,573 over 4 Years'. *Washington Post*. 24 January. https://www.washingtonpost.com/politics/2021/01/24/trumps-false-or-misleading-claims-total-30573-over-four-years/. Accessed 13 August 2024.

Kleinman, A. (1988). *The Illness Narratives*. New York: Basic Books.

Kuhn, A. (1995). *Family Secrets: Acts of Memory and Imagination*. London: Verso.

Labov, W. (1972). *Language in the Inner City: Studies in the Black English Vernacular*. Oxford: Basil Blackwell.

Labov, W. (1997). 'Some Further Steps in Narrative Analysis'. *Journal of Narrative and Life History* 7 (1–4): 395–415.

Labov, W., and J. Waletsky (1967). 'Narrative Analysis: Oral Versions of Personal Experience'. In J. Helms (ed.). *Essays in the Verbal and Visual Arts*, pp. 12–44. Seattle: University of Washington.

Lakhani, N. (2022). '"Africa Is on the Frontlines but Not on the Front Pages": Vanessa Nakate on Her Climate Fight'. *Guardian*. 26 September. https://www.theguardian.com/environment/2022/sep/17/vanessa-nakate-climate-activist-africa-cop27. Accessed 5 October 2023.

Langford, M. (2001). *Suspended Conversations: The Afterlife of Memory in Photograph Albums*. Montreal/London: McGill University Press.

Lapper, A. (2006). *My Life in My Hands*. London: Pocket Books.

Leaver, T., T. Highfield and C. Abidin (2020). *Instagram: Visual Social Media Cultures*. London: Wiley.

Lounasmaa, A., I. Esenowo and OLIve students (2019). 'Education Is Key to Life: The Importance of Education from the Point of View of Displaced Learners'. *Forced Migration Review* 60: 40–3.

Lounasmaa, A., C. Esin and C. Hughes (2020). "Decolonisation, Representation, and Ethics in Visual Life Stories from the Jungle". In S. Dodd (ed.). *Ethics and Integrity in Visual Research Methods (Advances in Research Ethics and Integrity, Vol. 5)*, pp. 11–28. Leeds: Emerald. https://doi.org/10.1108/S2398-601820200000005004.

Lounasmaa, A., E. Masserano, S. Quintero, Kim, Charles, J. Mordi, T. Makuyana, E. Achola and A. Fernando (2024). 'Writing Collaboratively in a Lockdown: Building Connections in Online Writing Groups with Refugees, Migrants and Local Communities.' In L. Moran and Z. Dooly (eds). *Biographical Perspectives on Lives Lived during Covid-19, Global Narratives and International Methodological Innovations 11*, Chapter 18, pp. 361–84. https://doi.org/10.1007/978-3-031-54442-2_18.

Lueg, K., and M. W. Lundholt (eds) (2021). *Routledge Handbook of Counter-Narratives*. London: Routledge.

Luttrell, W. (2020). *Children Framing Childhoods*. Bristol: Policy Press.

Lykes, B. (2021). 'Living Lives of Resistance in Multiple Registers: Dialogic Co-constructions, Genocidal Violence and Post-genocide Transitional Justice'. In C. Squire (ed.). *Stories Changing Lives*. New York: Oxford University Press.

Lyndon, S., and B. Edwards (2022). Beyond Listening: The Value of Co-research in the Co-construction of Narratives'. *Qualitative Research* 22 (4): 613–31.

Lyon, E. (2000). 'Biographical Constructions of a Working Woman'. *European Journal of Social Theory* 3 (2): 407–28.

Macintyre, A. (1984). *After Virtue*. Indiana: Notre Dame University Press.

Madisson, M., and A. Ventsel (2020). *Strategic Conspiracy Narratives: A Semiotic Approach*. London: Routledge.

Makela, M. and H. Meretoja (2022). 'Critical Approaches to the Storytelling Boom'. *Poetics Today* 43 (2): pp. 191–218.

Masserano, E., A. Lounasmaa, E. P. Achola, A. Fernando, P. L. Goba, P. Makuyana, J. Mordi and J. L. Phantsi (2021). 'Transformative Storytelling without Borders: The Case of OLIve'. *Sociological Observer* 2 (1) (published by the Sociological Association of Ireland https://www.sociol ogy.ie/publi cati ons.html).

Mayes, E. (2019). 'The Mis/uses of "Voice" in (Post)qualitative Research with Children and Young People: Histories, Politics and Ethics'. *International Journal of Qualitative Studies in Education* 32 (10): 1191–209.

Mbembe, A. (2015). 'Decolonising Knowledge and the Question of the Archive'. Witwatersrand University, WISER. https://wiser.wits.ac.za/sys tem/files/Achi lle%20Mbe mbe%20-%20D ecol oniz ing%20Kn owle dge%20and%20the%20Q uest ion%20of%20the%20Arch ive.pdf. Accessed 29 June 2024.

McAdams, D. (2006). *The Redemptive Self*. New York: Oxford University Press.

McAdams, D. (2021). '"First We Invented Stories, Then They Changed Us": The Evolution of Narrative Identity'. *Evolutionary Studies in Imaginative Culture* 3 (1): 1–18. https://www.degruyter.com/document/doi/10.26613/esic.3.1.110/html. Accessed 6 October 2023.

Meretoja, H. (2018). *The Ethics of Storytelling*. New York: Oxford University Press.

Meretoja, H., and C. Davis (eds) (2018). *Storytelling and Ethics: Literature, Visual Arts and the Power of Narrative*. London: Routledge.

Meretoja, H., and M. Freeman (eds) (2023). *The Use and Abuse of Stories: New Directions in Narrative Hermeneutics*. New York: Oxford University Press.

Mertova, P. (2019). *Using Narrative Inquiry as a Research Method: An Introduction to Critical Event Narrative Analysis in Research, Teaching and Professional Practice*. London: Routledge.

Miller, D. (2021). *Home Possessions*. London: Routledge.

Miller, P., and L. Sperry (1988). 'Early Talk about the Past: The Origins of Conversational Stories of Personal Experience'. *Journal of Child Language* 15: 293–315.

Mishler, E. (1986/1995). *Research Interviewing: Context and Narrative*. Cambridge, MA: Harvard University Press.

Mitchell, C., N. de Lange, and R. Molestane (2017). *Participatory Visual Methodologies: Social Change, Community and Policy*. London: Sage.

Moen, T. (2006). 'Reflections on the Narrative Research Approach'. *International Journal of Qualitative Methods* 5 (4): 56–69.

Moraga, C. (2015). *This Bridge Called My Back*. Binghamton, NY: Suny Press.

Morson, G. (1994). *Narrative and Freedom: The Shadows of Time*. New Haven, CT: Yale University Press.

Mulubale, S. (2020). 'Understanding the Seriousness of "Self" Identity and the Changing Process of HIV among Zambian School Teachers Living with Antiretroviral Therapy (ART)'. *Athens Journal of Health and Medical Sciences* 7 (4): 197–21.

Nacher, A. (2021). '#BlackProtest from the Web to the Streets and Back: Feminist Digital Activism in Poland and Narrative Potential of the Hashtag'. *European Journal of Women's Studies* 28 (2): 260–73.

Nagel, T. (1989). *The View from Nowhere*. New York: Oxford University Press.

Nakate, V. (2021). *A Bigger Picture*. London: One Boat.

Nakate, V. (2022). 'Vanessa Nakate's Remarks at Her Appointment as a UNICEF Goodwill Ambassador'. https://www.unicef.org/press-releases/vanessa-nakates-remarks-her-appointment-unicef-goodwill-ambassador. Accessed 5 October 2023.

Namiba, A., C. Niyermbe, M. Sachikonye, R. Mbewe and W. Ssanyu-Sseruma (2023). *Our Stories Told By Us*. London: ZZUK Press.

Nayeri, D. (2019). *The Ungrateful Refugee: What Immigrants Never Tell You*. Edinburgh: Canongate books.

Ndlovu, S. (2012). '"I Am More (than Just) Black": Contesting Multiplicity through Conferring and Asserting Singularity in Narratives of Blackness'. In R. Jossellson and M. Harway (eds). *Navigating Multiple Identities*, pp. 143–66. New York: Oxford University Press.

Ndlovu-Gatsheni, S. (2015). 'Decoloniality as the Future of Africa'. *History Compass* 13 (10): 485–96.

Newman, P., A. Guta and T. Black (2021). 'Ethical Considerations for Qualitative Research Methods during the COVID-19 Pandemic and Other Emergency Situations: Navigating the Virtual Field'. *International Journal of Qualitative Methods*. 20: 1–12.

Ngũgĩ wa Thiong'o (1938/1986). *Decolonising the Mind: The Politics of Language in African Literature*. London: Portsmouth. Currey; Heinemann.

Nhemachena, A., N. Mlamo and M. Kaundjua (2016). 'The Notion of the "Field" and the Practices of Researching and Writing Africa'. *Africology* 9 (7): 15–36.

Ochs, E., and L. Capps (2001). *Living Narrative: Creating Lives in Everyday Storytelling*. Cambridge: Harvard University Press.

O'Connor, P. (2000). *Speaking about Crime: Narratives of Prisoners*. Lincoln: University of Nebraska Press.

O'Neil, M., and B. Roberts (2020). *Walking Methods*. London: Routledge.

Överlien, C., and M. Hydén (2003). 'Work Identity at Stake: The Power of Sexual Abuse Stories in the World of Compulsory Youth Care'. *Narrative Inquiry* 13: 217–42.

Överlien, C., and M. Hydén. (2009). 'Children's Actions When Experiencing Violence'. *Childhood* 16: 479–96.

Page, R. (2018). *Narratives Online: Shared Stories in Social Media*. Cambridge: Cambridge University Press.

Papademas, D. (2009). 'IVSA Code of Research Ethics and Guidelines'. *Visual Studies* 24: 250–7.

Patel, G., and J. Spivey (2020). 'Against the "Good" Translation: The Power of Disobedience'. *Words Without Borders*. 1 September 2020, available at https://wordswithoutborders.org/read/article/2020-09/against-the-good-translation-the-power-of-disobedience-shadow-heroes/. Accessed 2 October 2023.

Patterson, W. (2013). 'Narratives of Events: Labovian Narrative Analysis and Its Limitations'. In M. Andrews, C. Squire and M. Tamboukou (eds). *Doing Narrative Research*, pp. 22–40. London: Sage.
Personal Narratives Group (1989). *Interpreting Women's Lives*. Bloomington: Indiana University Press.
Peterson, B. (2019). 'Spectrality and Inter-Generational Black Narratives in South Africa'. *Social Dynamics* 45 (3): 345–64.
Phoenix, A. (2013). 'Analysing Narrative Contexts'. In M. Andrews, C. Squire and M. Tamboukou (eds). *Doing Narrative Research*, pp. 64–77. London: Sage.
Phoenix, A. (2022). '(Re)-Inspiring Narratives of Resistance: COVID-19, Racisms and Narratives of Hope'. *Social Sciences* 11 (10): 470.
Phoenix, A. (2023). 'Making Diversity Visible in Often Unrecognised Family Practices'. *Families, Relationships and Societies* 12 (1): 31–48.
Phoenix, A., J. Brannen and C. Squire (2020). *Researching Family Narratives*. London: Sage.
Pizzey, E. (1974). *Scream Quietly or the Neighbors Will Hear*. Harmondsworth: Penguin.
Plummer, K. (1995). *Telling Sexual Stories: Power, Change and Social Worlds*. New York: Routledge.
Plummer, K. (2001). *Documents of Life 2*. London: Routledge.
Plummer, K. (2019). *Narrative Power: The Struggle for Human Value*. Cambridge: Polity Press.
Polkinghorne, D. (1988). *Narrative Knowing and the Human Sciences*. Albany, NY: State University of New York Press.
Polletta, F. (2006). *It Was Like a Fever*. Chicago, IL: University of Chicago Press.
Portelli, A. (2010). *They Say in Harlan County*. Oxford: Oxford University Press.
Propp, V. (1928/1968). *Morphology of the Folk Tale*. Austin: University of Texas Press.
Prosser, J., R. Clark and R. Wiles (2008). *Visual Research Ethics at the Crossroads*. NCRM Working Paper, Realities, Morgan Centre, Manchester, UK.
Ratele, K. (2019). *The World Looks Like This from Here*. Johannesburg: Wits University Press.
Rich, M., and R. Chalfen (1998). 'Showing and Telling Asthma: Children Teaching Physicians with Visual Narrative'. *Visual Sociology* 14: 51–71.
Ricoeur, P. (1984). *Time and Narrative*. Chicago, IL: University of Chicago Press.
Riessman, C. (1993). *Narrative Analysis: Qualitative Research Methods Series 30*. Newbury Park, CA: Sage.

Riessman, C. (2005). 'Exporting Ethics: A Narrative about Narrative Research in South India'. *Health* 9 (4): 473–90.

Riessman, C. (2008). *Narrative Methods for the Human Sciences*. New York: Sage.

Rogers, R. (2019). *Doing Digital Methods*. London: Sage.

Romm, N. (2020). 'Reflections on a Post-Qualitative Inquiry with Children/Young People: Exploring and Furthering a Performative Research Ethics'. *Forum: Qualitative Social Research* 21 (1): Art. 6.

Rose, G. (2022). *Visual Methodologies*. London: Sage. 5th Edition.

Ryan, M.-L. (2004). *Narrative across Media: The Languages of Storytelling*. Lincoln: University of Nebraska Press.

Ryan, M.-L. (2022). *A New Anatomy of Storyworlds*. Columbus: Ohio State University Press.

Sarbin, T. (1986). *Narrative Psychology: The Storied Nature of Human Conduct*. New York: Praeger.

Schegloff, E. (1997). 'Narrative Analysis: Thirty Years Later'. *Journal of Narrative and Life History* 7: 41–52.

Schiff, B. (2017). *A New Narrative for Psychology*. New York: Oxford University Press.

Scott, J. C. (1990). *Domination and the Arts of Resistance: Hidden Transcripts*. New London, CT: Yale University Press.

Scott, J. C. (1992). 'Experience'. In J. Butler and J. Scott (eds). *Feminists Theorise the Political*, pp. 22–40. New York: Routledge.

Seale, C. (2004). 'Resurrective Practice and Narrative'. In M. Andrews, S. D. Sclater, C. Squire and A. Treacher (eds). *Lines of Narrative*, pp. 36–47. London: Routledge.

Selbin, E. (2010). *Revolution, Rebellion, Resistance: The Power of Story*. London: Zed Books.

Sermijn, J., G. Loots and P. Devlieger (2010). 'Wolves in Sheep's Clothing or Sheep in Wolf's Clothing?' *Creative Approaches to Research* 3 (2): 39–51.

Shaw, R., J. Howe, J. Beazer and T. Carr (2020). 'Ethics and Positionality in Qualitative Research with Vulnerable and Marginal Groups'. *Qualitative Research* 20 (3): 277–93.

Sheringham, O., and H. Taylor (2022). 'On Stories, Storytelling, and the Quiet Politics of Welcome'. *ACME: An International E-Journal for Critical Geographies* 21 (3): 284–302.

Soundy, A. (2018). 'Psycho-Emotional Content of Illness Narrative Master Plots for People with Chronic Illness'. *World Journal of Psychiatry* 8 (3): 79–82.

Spivak, G. (1988). 'Can the Subaltern Speak?'. In C. Nelson and L. Grossberg (eds). *Marxism and the Intepretation of Culture*, pp. 267–310. Chicago, IL: University of Chicago Press.

Spivak, G. C. (2012). 'The Politics of Translation'. In L. Venuti (ed.). *The Translation Studies Reader*, pp. 312–30. Abingdon, England: Routledge.
Squire, C. (2007). *Talking about the Big Thing*. London: Methuen
Squire, C. (2013). *Living with HIV and ARVs: Three-Letter Lives*. London: Palgrave.
Squire, C. (2021). *Stories Changing Lives*. New York: Oxford University Press.
Squire, C. (2024). 'Dominant and Counteracting Narratives of "Crisis" in COVID Times.' In M. Dege and I. Strasser (eds). *Narrative in Crisis*, Chapter 4, pp. 49–70. New York: Oxford University Press.
Squire, C., M. Davis, C. Esin, B. Harrison, L. C. Hyden and M. Hyden (2014). *What Is Narrative Research?* London: Bloomsbury.
Squire, C., and JB de Lemos (2022). 'Narrating Resistant Citizenships through Two Pandemics'. *Social Sciences* 11 (8): 358.https://doi.org/10.3390/socsci11080358.
Squire, C., C. Esin and C. Burman (2013). '"You Are Here": Visual Autobiographies, Cultural-Spatial Positioning, and Resources for Urban Living'. *Sociological Research Online* 18 (3): 1–18. http://www.socresonline.org.uk/18/3/1.html.
Stanley, L. (1995). *The Auto/biographical I*. Manchester: Manchester University Press.
Tamboukou, M. (2010). *Nomadic Narratives, Visual Forces: Gwen John's Letters and Paintings*. New York: Peter Lang.
Tamboukou, M. (2013). 'A Foucauldian Approach to Narratives'. In M. Andrews, C. Squire and M. Tamboukou (eds). *Doing Narrative Research*, Chapter 4, pp. 102–20, 2nd edn. London: Sage.
Tamboukou, M. (2018). *Women Workers' Education, Life Narratives and Politics: Geographies, Histories, Pedagogies*. London: Palgrave Macmillan.
Temple, B., and K. Koterba (2009). 'The Same but Different: Researching Language and Culture in the Lives of Polish People in England'. *Forum: Qualitative Social Research* 10 (1).
Thomas, W., and F. Znaniecki (1918–20). *The Polish Peasant in Europe and America*. Chicago, IL and Boston, MA: University of Chicago Press and Badger Press.
Todorov, T. (1990). *Genres in Discourse*. Cambridge: Cambridge University Press.
Tolich, M., and E. Tumilty (2020). 'Practicing Ethics and Ethics Praxis'. *Qualitative Report* 25 (13): 16–30.
Torre, M. E., M. Fine, K. Boudin, I. Bowen and J. Clark (2001). 'A Space for Co-constructing Counter Stories under Surveillance". *International Journal of Critical Psychology* (4): 149–66.

Treisman, R. (2022). 'Putin's Claim of Fighting Ukraine "neo-Nazis" Distorts History, Scholars Say.' https://www.npr.org/2022/03/01/1083677765/putin-denazify-ukraine-russia-history. 1 March. Accessed 13 August 2024.

Trott, V. (2021). 'Networked Feminism: Counterpublics and the Intersectional Issues of #MeToo', *Feminist Media Studies* 21 (7): 1125–42.

Tuck, E., and K. Wayne Yang (2014). 'R-words: Refusing Research'. In D. Paris and M. Winn (eds). *Humanizing Research*, pp. 223–48. London: Sage.

Tuhiwai Smith, L. (1999). *Decolonising Methodologies*. London: Zed Press.

Turkle, S. (2007). *Evocative Objects: Things We Think With*. Cambridge, MA: MIT Press.

Vacchelli, E. (2018). *Embodied Research in Migration Studies: Using Creative and Participatory Methods*. Bristol and Chicago: Policy Press

Vetere, A., and E. Dowling (2005). *Narrative Therapies with Children and Their Families*. London: Routledge.

Walkerdine, V. (1991). 'Behind the Painted Smile'. In J. Spence and P. Holland (eds). *Family Snaps: The Meaning of Domestic Photography*, pp. 35–45. London: Virago.

Wells, K. (2013). 'The Melodrama of Being a Child'. *Visual Communication* 12 (3): 277–93.

Wengraf, T. (2019). 'Researching Dated, Situated Subjectivities by Biographic-Narrative Interview'. In K. Stamenova and R. Hinshelwood (eds). *Methods of Research into the Unconscious*, Chapter 12, pp. 211–38. London: Routledge.

White, M., and D. Epson (1990). *Narrative Means to Therapeutic Ends*. New York: Norton.

Wigginton, E. (ed.) (1992). *Refuse to Stand Silently By: An Oral History of Grass Roots Social Activism in America*. New York: Doubleday.

Wilkomirski, B. (1997). *Fragments: Memories of a Childhood (1939–1948)*. London: Picador.

Wilson, S. (2001). *Research Is Ceremony: Indigenous Research Methods*. Halifax, NS: Fernwood.

Wright Mills, C. (1959). *The Sociological Imagination*. London: Oxford University Press.

Yang, M. (2002). 'Articulate Image, Painted Diary: Frida Kahlo's Autobiographical Interface'. In S. Smith and J. Watson (eds). *Interfaces*, pp. 314–41. Ann Arbor: University of Michigan Press.

Yardley, S., R. Kinston, J. Lefroy, S. Gay and R. McKinley (2020). '"What Do We *Do*, Doctor?" Transitions of Identity and Responsibility: A Narrative Analysis'. *Advances in Health Science Education* 25: 825–43.

Zingaro, L. (2009). *Speaking Out: Storytelling for Social Change*. Walnut Creek, CA: Left Coast Press.

INDEX

Abdi, M. 22, 26, 38, 109
activity narratives 14, 63, 77, 108, 115, 124
Adichie, C. 8
Ahmed, S. 96
Alam, S. 2
Alwan, N. A. 44
Andrews, M. 77, 93
anti-colonial 25–6
anti-positivism 20
Anzaldúa, G. 35
Association of Narrative Research and Practice 2
audiovisual narratives 13, 108
autobiographical stories 22, 47, 87, 94, 98
autobiographies 44, 53

backshadowing 32. *See also* sideshadowing
Baele, S. 7
Baker, M. 34
Bamberg, M. 38
Barthes, R. 18
battered woman 61–5
Bell, S. 53
Berger, J. 52
Bernstein, M. A. 32
Bhabha, H. 9
big stories 15, 51. *See also* small stories
Biographic-Narrative Interpretive Method (BNIM) 88

biology, and narratives 20
#BlackLivesMatter 75, 90
Blaike, J. 76
body narratives 13, 55
body positioning in narrative 47
Boonzaier, F. 2, 6, 23, 26, 105, 108
bottom-up (inductive approaches) 15
Brannlund, E. 34
Brevik, A. 41
Bruner, J. 11, 21, 57, 94
Bury, M. 98
Butler, J. 94

Cambridge Analytica scandal 58
Capps, L. 33
Cardinal, T. 22–3, 89, 92
Carney, S. 39
Carolissen, R. 24
Carver, N. 12
Casualty 97
Cavanagh, S. 117
Cavieres-Fernandez, E. 39
authenticity of narratives 123–6
challenges in narrative research 105–26. *See also* narrative research
different kinds of data and analysis 113–15
difficulty of narrative materials 111–13
ethical complexities 120–3

feeding back findings to participants 118–19
presenting research findings 116–18
unavailability of research instructions 105–11
chaos narratives 86, 89, 96, 98
Charon, R. 98
children 51
  abuse of 60
  climate emergency 6, 7
  food relief for 26
  mind the women and 30
  parents tell stories together with 33
  stories of witnessing violence 66–7
  supporting through storytelling 33
Chilean teachers' narratives 39
co-construction/co-constructed 29–31, 59, 60, 92, 114
cognition, and narratives 20
coherence 3. *See also* incoherence of narratives 31–4
Colston, E. 75
community contract 22, 26
complicating action 16
computer game 2, 7
constructionism 8, 106
constructionist approach 8, 86, 106, 107
content-based narrative research 23
contextual analysis 11
conversational stories 33
conversational storytelling 33, 133. *See also* storytelling
conversation analysis 13
counter-narrative(s) 38–41, 51, 71
  of multiculturalism 34
Covid-19 44, 51, 94, 96, 98, 100, 116, 122

criminology 2, 26
critical humanist narrative approach 21
critical race theory 38
Crow, G. 53
cultural studies 2, 10, 18
cultural theory 18

Davis, M. 93, 95, 109, 114
Davison, E. 75
decoloniality/decolonial 26
De Fina, A. 55
De Lemos, J.B. 96
Del Tufo, A. 23, 87, 89, 92
dialogic narratives 30–1, 101
dialogue and co-construction 29–31
diaries 99, 108, 113
  video diary 49
digital narratives 44
discourse 11
  analysis 10, 18
  approach 68
  of power and knowledge 19
domestic abuse and violence 60
dominant narrative. *See* master narratives

effective activism 78
Elliott, J. 8, 86
emancipatory research 49
embodiment, and storytelling 45
Emergency: NYC 97
emotional narratives 13
emotions 46
Enlightenment 21
epistemic oppression 25
epistemology 24
Esin, C. 36, 53, 68, 93, 95, 109, 110, 111
ethical hesitancy 36
ethics, narrative research 120
evaluative material 16

INDEX

event narratives 16, 17
   vs. topic narratives 101
everyday narrative 15, 49
experiential 22, 57

fabula 30–1. *See also* story
Facebook 55, 58
fairy tales 16
family story 14
Fernandes, S. 35
film theory 2
Fine, M. 39
fine art 2
Flickr 51
Flowers, P. 95
Floyd, G. 40
Flying Doctors 97
foreshadowing 32. *See also* backshadowing
Foucauldian discourse approach 68
Foucault, M. 21, 63, 67, 68
'found' photographs 50
Frank, A. 86, 89, 96, 98, 99
Freeman, M. 78
Frye, N. 21

Gates, H. L. 38
gay 82, 94, 117
   ethnic minority 57
   marriage 39
   rights and civil rights 25
Gee, J. 20
gender 36
   narratives of 69
gender-based violence 60
generation 53, 67, 70, 87, 93, 95, 107
Genette, G. 18
genre 9, 21, 96
Georgakopoulou, A. 56
gestures 46
Giaxoglu, K. 56
Glasgow Rent Strike 79

Good, B. 98
Greenhalgh, T. 98

Hage, G. 96
Hammack, P. B. 57
Harper, D. 50
Harris, A. 39
Harrison, B. 109, 111
#hashtag activism 56, 57
Hawkins, A. 98, 99
health and illness 97–101
Heart, S. E. 25, 26, 91
Herman, D. 15, 91
history 2, 10, 18
humanist 20
Hitler, A. 79
HIV narratives 22, 23, 57, 83–5, 94, 96–7, 99, 111, 115–16.
   See also illness narratives
Hospital Playlist 97
humanist psychology 20–1
Hurwitz, B. 98
Hydén, L.-C. 111
Hydén, M. 45, 62, 95, 110–12
Hyden. L.C. 45
hypertextual narratives 15
Hyvarinen, M. 39

identity 37, 63
   construction 107
   HIV 84
   markers 36
   personal 6
   politics 94
   self-identity 95
illness
   and health 97–101
   narratives 89, 96–100
incoherence 3, 10, 31, 33. *See also* coherence
Instagram 50, 51, 55, 56
internet-based narrative
   communication 117

intertextualities 15, 20
interview narratives 13, 15
intimate stories 94

Jaworska, S. 57
#JeSuisCharlie 90
John, G. 50

Ka Canham, H. 23–4, 91
Kahlo, F. 50
Kasadha, B. 25
Kavelina, D. 62, 87, 91
Kerrigan, Rose 77–8
Kessi, S. 53
Kiguwa, P. 24
Kleinman, A. 98–9
Kuhn, A. 51

Labov, W. 16–18, 20, 86, 115
Langford, M. 50, 53
Lapper, A., 44
letters 50, 99, 106, 108, 113
Lévi-Strauss, C. 18
life course 87
life narrative 15, 94
life stories 40, 63, 87, 90–1, 92, 128, 133
linguistics analysis 13
listeners 47
   and narrators 55
   and storytellers 33, 44–5
   and tellers 45, 46, 48
literary studies 2
literary theory 21
lived experience 57–8, 84, 86, 87, 89, 92, 97–9, 115
Livermore, M. 63
Lohm, D. 93, 109, 114
Lounasmaa, A. 36, 90, 93
Luttrell, W. 14, 53

MacIntyre, A. 94
macro-narratives 68–71
macro political narratives 74
management 2, 82
Marx, K. 75
Masserano, E. 93
master narratives 38–40, 58, 71
media narratives 10, 14
mega policy narrative 39
memories 46, 52
Meretoja, H. 123
#MeToo movement 60, 90
micro-narratives 68–71
Miller, P. 33
Mills, C.W. 20, 75
Mishler, E. 98
Mohr, J. 52
Montgomery Bus Boycott 75, 79
Morson, G. S. 32
moving-image narratives 49
Mpondo theory 23, 91
multilinguality and
   translation 34–5

Nacher, A. 57
Nakate, V. 4–7, 9–10, 14, 17, 22, 26, 30, 32–7, 89, 91, 94, 95, 96, 97
Namiba, A. 22–3, 25–6, 94, 97
narrative analysis 12, 18, 19, 44, 68, 70, 71, 106, 107, 110, 112, 114–15
narrative analysis, participant feedback 118
narrative as resource 8–9
narrative as theme 8–9
narrative body 46
narrative content 10–12
narrative context 10–12, 14, 18–19
narrative criminology 26
narrative inquiry 22, 89, 92
narrative medicine 100
narrative methods, steps 106
narrative research 1–2, 4, 7, 8, 16–21

Index

approaches 12
and the body 44–8
challenges in 105–26
   (*see* challenges in narrative research)
contemporary issues in 29–41
   coherence of narratives 31–4
   counter-narrative 38–41
   dialogue and co-construction 29–31
   reflexivity of narratives 36–8
   story and narrative, distinction between 29–31
   translation and multilinguality 34–5
ethics 120
on interpersonal violence 63
in investigations of violence and abuse 59–67
political effects of 26
social justice and re-humanization 21–7
uses of 81–103
   (*see* uses of narrative research)
narrative researchers 6, 11, 13, 63, 71, 88, 102
   role of 8–12, 15
narrative(s) 2, 12–16
   of the 1960s 23
   counter-narratives 38–41, 51, 71
   defined 4–5
   gender-based violence 1, 60
   of generation 93
   illness 98–101
   macro and micro 68–71
   phenomenological approach to 21
   political effects of 26
   political narratives 73–9
   progressive histories of 26
   as sense-making tools 78
   of sexualities and power 67–73
   signs of 4–5, 7
   social and historical limitations 5
   and social media 54–8
   in social research 20, 37–57, 59–79
   as specific phenomena 5
   and story, distinction between 29–31
   truth of 8, 123
   unconscious 19
   visual narratives 14, 48–57
   voice 82–5
narratives analysis 7
narratives and sensitive topics. *See* uses of narrative research
narrative structure 9, 14, 17, 18, 55, 86, 110
narrative thematic analysis 10
narrative voice 84–5
narratology 10
naturalism 8, 106
neurological narratives 20
Ngũgĩ wa Thiong'o 35
normative multiculturalism 41

object narratives 13, 14, 24. *See also* narrative(s)
Ochs, E. 33
O'Connor, P. 60
ontology 24, 107
oral narratives 13, 98

painting 49, 50
paralinguistic narratives 13
Parks, R. 75–8
performance 10, 48, 51, 57, 82, 89, 92, 106, 107, 117
personal narratives 9, 14, 57
phenomenological approach 21
phenomenology 88
Phoenix, A. J. 6, 82
photo elicitation 50
photograph-sharing sites 51
photography 1, 110
photo-voice 49, 50

164 INDEX

Plummer, K. 8, 25, 60, 68, 86, 94
political narratives 73–9
Polletta, F. 90–2, 94
polysemy 19
positioning 19, 24, 41, 47, 67, 68, 95, 109, 112, 124, 131
   of the body 46
   in construction of sexual stories 71–3
positivism 106
postmodernism 18, 21
poststructuralism 18, 21
pragmatic narrative research 12
process narratives 14
programmatic narrative research 12
Propp, V. 16
psychoanalytic studies 2
Putin, V. 79

quest narratives 89
Quintero, S. 35, 87, 89

reading images 53
recordings 5, 6, 13, 45
reflexivity 36–8, 59, 112
re-humanization 21–7
resource, narratuive as 8–9
restitution narratives 89
Ricoeur, P. 21, 88
Riessman, C.K. 34, 105, 111
romanticization 84
Rushdie, S. 56
Ryan, M.-L. 91

Saussure, F. de 18
Scott, J. C. 63
selfhood 11
self-narrative 95
sensitive topics 101–3, 111
Sermijn, J. 117
sexualities and power 67–73
sexual modesty 68

sexual stories 60, 71–3
sexual violence and abuse 59–67
sideshadowing 32. *See also* backshadowing
small stories 15, 18. *See also* big stories
social change 22, 25, 38, 93–4
social constructionist approaches 86, 88
social exclusion 85, 120
sociality 25, 87, 95–6
social justice 21–7
social media narratives 54–8
   and lived experience 57–8
   meanings and effects of 56–7
   structural analyses of 55–6
social networks 65–6
social research 87
   stories 45
social theory 18
socio-legal studies 2
sound narratives 13
South African Truth and Reconciliation Commission 115
Spivak, G. C. 35
spoken narratives 5, 13
Squire, C. 53, 90, 96, 98
still image narratives 13
story and narrative, distinction between 29–31
story(ies) 4–6, 11, 15, 17, 19, 25–7
   autobiographical 47
   of children witnessing violence 66–7
   and family 14
   intimate 94
   and narrative, distinction between 6, 29–31
   small 18
   of social networks' responses 65–6
   social research 45

truthful 9
types of 60–1
storytellers 3, 11, 39, 45, 47, 71, 73, 92, 103, 113
storytelling 10–11, 25, 94
 conversational 33, 133
 and embodiment 45
 multilingual 35
 and social media 56
 supporting children through 33
storyworlds 15
structural linguistics 16, 18, 23
structure 9, 11, 17, 21, 25, 32, 35, 38, 55, 62, 75, 86, 88, 90, 106, 107, 110, 125
subaltern knowledge 38
subjectivities 18, 19, 23, 32, 88
supported storytelling 33
syuzhet 30–1

Tamboukou, M. 50
tellers and listener 46, 48, 101
thematic narrative analysis 7, 10, 12, 32, 86, 108
theme, narrative as 8–9
theory-method 24
Thomas, W., 20
TikTok 51, 55
Todorov, T. 18
top-down (deductive approaches) 15
Torre, M. E. 39
transcription 13, 23, 45, 46
transcripts 13, 45, 63, 109, 117
translation and multilinguality 34–5
transmedial narratives 15
transmodality 20
Trott, V. 57
truth
 of narratives 8–9, 123–6
 relativistic exploration of multiple 24
Turkish modernization 68, 93
24 hours in A&E 97

unconscious, the 19, 21. *See also* narratives
unconscious narratives 13
UNICEF 95, 96
uses of narrative research 81–103. *See also* narrative research
 exploration of little-known phenomena and narrative voice 82–5
 understanding health and illness 97–101
 understanding lives 86–92
 understanding narratives in relation to social, cultural and political contexts 93–7
 understanding sensitive topics and sensitive events 101–3

video diaries 49
video-sharing sites 51
violence observed by children 66–7
visual autobiographies 53
visual counter-narratives 51
visual narratives 14, 48–57
visual social media platforms 50
voice 45, 82–5

Waletsky, J. 20
Walkerdine, V. 51
Weinstein, H. 40, 60
Wells, H. G., 15
Wells, K. 96
Wipff, Z. 38
World War II 79
written narratives 13, 32, 87

X (Twitter) 51

YouTube 50

Zelensky, V. 79
Zoom 55